Intersecting Voices

Intersecting Voices

Women Who Write

Beneath the Peak

Story Preserves, LLC
Denver, Colorado
www.storypreserves.com

Cover designed by Rosemary Scheuering
Painting of Pikes Peak on cover by Rosemary Scheuering

Library of Congress Control Number: 2015915014
ISBN-13: 978-1-943324-02-6
ISBN-10: 1943324026

We dedicate this book to the women
who have come before.
Pioneer women who had the courage to
venture across vast areas of the new world
under the most trying circumstances.
Women who gave birth to the first generation
of American citizens born on native soil.
Women who plowed the fields
and nursed their families.
Suffragettes who through their tenacity
gave women the right to vote
despite being harassed and jailed.
Women who became leaders in politics
and worked for the good of mankind.
Women who won the Nobel Prize
for their outstanding research
and contributions.
Women who impacted history.
Women who made a difference.
And to the Women
whose voices have not been heard.

Irmgard von der Gathen

Write what should not be forgotten.

Isabel Allende

Contents

Introduction

Intersecting Voices is the offspring of a writers' interest group sponsored by the Colorado Springs branch of American Association of University Women (AAUW). A group of women with diverse backgrounds, we share the common goal of finding our literary voices.

When we started this project, each of us had the desire to write, and a few of us already had the enthusiasm and initiative to publish our thoughts and ideas. We came from everywhere, like the early settlers of the Pikes Peak region. One of our members is originally from Sweden, one from Germany; most of us were born in the U.S., but our home states are as diverse as our professions.

AAUW is one of the many things that these nineteen women have in common. The organization and its members are dedicated to improving conditions in our world—not only for women of the U.S. but for everyone. We hope that our support for women's education will have a far-reaching effect.

In coming together to mutually support our sisters in the craft of writing, we discovered that we were more than the sum of our individual efforts. The term "women who write" defines us as individuals with the ambition to leave a gift of ourselves to our families, friends and any others interested in our personal literary efforts. Even more significantly, the term signifies that we have joined the ranks of women writers who have shared their unique visions and experiences throughout history.

Since we formed our writing group, we have become strongly committed to learning more about each other and our personal journeys. Most importantly, we find that writing is a window into ourselves. We all give great thanks that we have found a trusting and friendly environment to compose stories that bring tears and laughter and "ah-ha" moments to us all.

When we share our writing efforts, we feel affirmed, and our writing draws us closer to each other. We encourage our readers, likewise, to connect with us through this collection of stories, memoirs, poems, and other thoughts. As we share these pages with you, our voices ring clear, each one distinctive and yet blended into the chorus of womanhood.

Jeanne Marsh

Shirley Miekka

Shirley was born in 1937, and grew up on a "sort-of farm" outside the sleepy town of Grand Blanc, Michigan, the youngest of three kids. She was rather shy, did well in school, and spent hours each day reading novels and practicing piano. But rather than literature or music, she chose science as her focus for college. She completed her undergraduate degree (pharmacy) at the University of Michigan/Ann Arbor, and then moved to the University of Wisconsin/Madison, where she earned a Ph.D. in physiological chemistry. While there, she developed a love of nature and outdoor activities—camping, canoeing, hiking, and skiing. After a few post-doctoral years doing research in Bern, Switzerland, Shirley returned to the U.S. and settled in the Maryland suburbs of Washington, D.C.

During the next 35 years she conducted laboratory research, first at the American Red Cross Blood Research Lab and later in small biotechnology start-ups. While there, she also explored alternative mind-body techniques (acupuncture, reiki, energy medicine) and became licensed in Educational Kinesiology (aka Brain Gym®). After retirement, she moved to Colorado Springs in 2009 to be close to family. She joined AAUW and started participating in the Women Who Write group. Meanwhile, she had become interested in Costa Rica, and built a house there, which serves as her vacation home. "I love the country, the people and the language!" she says. Shirley remained single all these years, but is quite contented with her life.

If I Could...

If I could be whatever I wanted to be, I would be beautiful, slender, happy and rich. I would have a loving, sexy husband, attractive, successful, doting children, adorable grandchildren and maybe some greats.

If I could, I would be like my friends in Women Who Write. I would be as artistic as Rosemary, as avant-garde and multitalented as Irmgard. I'd sing gorgeous harmonies as does Jeanne, be as stylish and beautiful as Phyllis. I'd make wild and interesting jewelry like Shirlea or create clever crafts and paintings like Marge. I'd write plays and act in the theater like Judith. I'd be as articulate as Joann. I'd travel to exotic destinations and present travelogues like Janet. I'd be as quietly witty and concise as Lani. I'd know *everyone*, as Dixie does. I'd be a sophisticated, published European like Chris and Irmgard. I'd be a sensitive advocate for victims of abuse as is Joyce A., and astute and politically involved as are Char and Cara. I'd travel the world with my close family like Joyce C. and June and be a gourmet chef like Corkie. I'd have a passel of talented grandchildren like my sister June.

I could go on and on, but why do that? Yes, I have talented, accomplished, lovely friends. But wouldn't it be better to celebrate them and enjoy their rich talents, than to envy them or want to be in their shoes? Let's face it, if I could I would, but I can't, so I won't fret about it.

I really *could* be happier in my own skin, though, and more accepting and appreciative of who I really am. No, I'm not beautiful or skinny or married or a parent. My artistic talents are buried inside, waiting for the day when I dare to express myself in paint or pen, just for the fun of it. My singing voice cracks at middle C, so I only sing in the shower or in vocal groups with limited requirements. My writing tends to be linear and autobiographical, not poetic or abstract or multimodal like that of my Women Who Write friends. Yes, I vote, but I am not politically involved or an advocate for the less fortunate. Yes, I travel, but almost always to the same place, my well-loved house in Costa Rica.

What do I do well—what am I most proud of? I think it is that my heart opens up to people. I can feel joy in seeing the beauty in the human beings with whom I share this space and time. I can see the talents and good hearts of my friends, family, neighbors, and even strangers. The people in my life give me pleasure by being different from me and different from one another.

And so if I could I would *not* choose to be talented in the same ways my friends are. Let me—let all of us—just enjoy the awareness of being unique, different from everyone else. Let's celebrate our marvelous diversity, as the French do when they say *Vive la difference!*

How to Weave a Poem

Beth Ann, the poet, tells us to free-write
for a while – we have 30 minutes.
Then, she says, go back and see your work
with fresh eyes and a clear mind.

There may be a poem interwoven there
among the freely-written words, she says;

Like an unexpected pattern woven into a fabric
on the loom of a weaver who, as she weaves,
lets her mind wander into wistful memories of
past loves, lost youth, fleeting joys or
bygone disappointments.

Only to discover, when she wakes,
she's changed her color palette to merge
more somber tones into her sun-bright plan.

She finds solace in the dark-streaked threads
intermingled within the sunny design –
A richer, deeper pattern that
reveals long forgotten secrets.
It pleases her eye and heart.

"I'll keep it this way" she says.

Wisdom and Insight

In December 2011, I had my routine mammogram. Unlike previous tests, this one was different. The radiologist called me into his office afterwards and said the images showed clusters of calcium deposits in my right breast, and I needed a biopsy. I didn't like the sound of that, but it was probably nothing—it usually was, I had heard.

I had the needle biopsy in January, just before I was scheduled to fly to Costa Rica for a six-week vacation. I asked the surgeon, Dr. Greene, if I should cancel or postpone my trip until the results were in. She said I could go, but I might have to return early if the results looked bad.

So I flew to Costa Rica to stay in my beautiful house in the central highlands. A week after I arrived, Dr. Greene called to tell me I had a type of breast cancer called DCIS, which stands for Ductile Carcinoma in Situ, meaning it was inside a milk duct. The good news: the DCIS was Stage 0, still contained within the duct. The bad news: it was a fast-growing cell type.

Not surprisingly, this changed my life. Suddenly I felt mortal—very mortal! Here I was in my Costa Rican paradise, and the sky was falling on my head! I made some calls to family and friends in search of relief from my distress. My cousin Joanne asked if I'd like to phone a psychic she knew in Denver. I had consulted psychics a few times in the past, and found it could sometimes be comforting. So I called Toby for an appointment. She tuned in with her "spirit guides" and told me many wonderful things about myself and my life. I received lots of encouraging support from her and the spirits, and they said I would survive this illness. The main message was I should remember what brings me joy, what I love to do, and bring that back into my life. The breast cancer was a "wake-up call" to help me get back on track; to make the years I have left as meaningful and joyful as possible.

I thought of one major thing this might mean. When I lived in the Washington D.C. area, I practiced a mind/body technique for many years called Educational Kinesiology (or Brain Gym), a way of using specific movements to integrate brain hemispheres and improve whole body function. The process can help people clarify their goals and overcome internal barriers or blocks to learning. Working with individuals was a wonderful experience for me and gave me a deep sense of calmness and peace. When I moved to Colorado Springs in 2009, it was harder for me to practice Brain Gym because there was no community of practitioners here. I was the only licensed instructor and after a few years I let my license expire through indecision, inaction and lack of support. There are other things that brought me joy in the past that I have stopped doing as well. I rarely dance to Latin rhythms, hardly ever play the piano, and never go camping. I don't go to the gym or do yoga to experience the joy of movement. I needed to change!

After I returned from Costa Rica I had the recommended cancer treatments—lumpectomy (twice) and radiation in the spring and summer of 2012. The treatments were successful and I have not had any evidence of cancer for three years and counting.

This is an unfinished story. It took me two years to reestablish my Brain Gym licensure. Although I still do not have an active practice, I have scheduled some introductory classes and hope to begin facilitating individual sessions. I have found a yoga class to join, and re-started at the gym. I got out some of my Chopin sheet music this week and am starting over on the piano. It is time to bring joy back into my life in small and large ways. After all, I don't want to receive a second wake-up call, one that could be more serious than the first one.

I am grateful to the cancer for bringing this message to me loud and clear. I truly believe this scary episode was a gift and a blessing. I know now that experiencing joy in my life is crucial for maintaining my health and well-being. It is amazing how something as menacing as cancer can bring wisdom and insight, showing me how to live life in a better way.

The Lake

We woke that Sunday morning to a crisp clear day. The sun shone brightly, the sky cloudless with no trace of wind. We knew it was somehow special and trudged out early to the lakeshore, bundled in wooly layers, skates draped over our shoulders.

What a glorious scene! The lake had frozen solid overnight, a sight we'd never seen before, smooth as glass and crystal clear, two inches deep, or maybe more. We walked out on the ice to gaze into the depths. Like glass, the ice hid nothing from our view. Schools of fish swam under us, darting away when startled by our unexpected shadows. Weeds swayed slowly, moved by unseen currents, tiny snails clinging to their grassy blades. I experienced the enchantment, the joy, of seeing Nature in a totally new light.

Later, with skates on, we glided across to the other shore. Lake Wingra is not so large, you know. It felt like flying, to skate on ice that smooth, everywhere crystal clear, mirroring the sun above and revealing the wonderland below.

How long did we revel in that glorious morning? Long enough to imprint its memory through 50 years or more, lived far from those beautiful Wisconsin shores.

Time Out of Mind

Time out of mind—what an odd expression! Where did it come from? What does it mean? Let me ponder some possibilities.

One idea is that *time out of mind* expresses a gigantic span of eons and eons, so immense the mind is unable to grasp its endless duration. It is so much time, we cannot wrap our minds around it. It is like the primal creation of our universe in the Big Bang, or the expansion of space indefinitely, until the end of time. Incomprehensible. Limitless. Everlasting.

Another idea is that time is *of the mind*, that it is created by the mind. Time is a linear sequential measurement of our existence in life. A way to quantify the interval between our birth and our death, breaking our lifetime down into years, seasons, months, days, hours, minutes, seconds, breaths, heart beats. Perhaps breaking our life down into measureable intervals gives us a grasp of life's passage, clarity into its meaning, a sense of control.

In terms of brain function, time measurement is usually accomplished by the left hemisphere, our logical, linear brain half. Time *matters* to the left brain. My left hemisphere, for one, is extremely adept at counting out seconds and minutes. I usually know what time it is without checking a clock. The right hemisphere has no interest in time. It pays no attention whatever to time's passage. So maybe the phrase should read *time out of right mind*.

OK, here's another one. My Costa Rican ("Tico") friends have very little concept of time. If I have an appointment for the Tico cable guy to come to my house to fix my TV or internet reception, and he says he'll come Tuesday at 8:00 a.m., he may mean Tuesday at dinnertime, or Thursday sometime, or maybe Tuesday next week or later. He never calls to say he will be late. What does "late" mean, anyway, for a *time-out-of-mind* guy? The technical term for this is Tico Time. How many days have I sat at home waiting for some Tico who never showed up? On the other hand, maybe to compensate, we gringos keep very precise time schedules (called Gringo Time). If I am going to be five minutes late for a meeting, I call ahead to warn my gringo friends, who thank me. My Tico friends think this is loco.

Finally, is *time out of mind* a spiritual concept having to do with eternity, the everlasting? An other-worldly place or state where time does not exist? The universe before the Big Bang? The timeless state of bliss reached by mystics in their deepest meditation or approach to Samadhi? Is it Heaven on earth, or Heaven after we depart this earth?

God only knows!

Charlotte Gagne

Charlotte Gagne was born in Walnut Creek, California, in the San Francisco Bay area. She graduated in 1971 with a BS in Home Economics education from Cal Poly, San Luis Obispo, California, and taught high school family consumer studies in Saratoga, California, until 1980. She obtained a Master's degree in Marriage, Child, and Family counseling from University of Santa Clara in 1979 and moved with her husband to Colorado Springs, Colorado, in 1980. In 1987, she earned a master's degree in Special Education from University of Colorado, Colorado Springs and taught learning disabled students at Air Academy High School in School District 20 for 20 years.

Her son, Douglas, was born in 1989 and thus she began the marathon of teaching, parenting, and juggling life's demands. Colorado has provided the outdoor, scenic beauty and quality of life sought after leaving congested California. Now that her son, a Boettcher scholar and gainfully employed tax-payer, is launched in life, Charlotte and her husband are retired, enjoying traveling, hiking, and engaging with like-minded friends through AAUW.

Cousins

Slender rivulets of sweat trickle down my brow, valley heat, always present in the summer. We can never just do ordinary when it comes to food. When did that arena become the major exposition, competition? So much energy goes into the preparations of what we eat, gone in 10 minutes, but oh, the praise, subtle badges of admiration we collect surreptitiously.

Car packed with boxes of food offerings, our suitcases hiding in the corner amidst coolers, bags. Another stop along the way to O'Briens, the fancy cheese and gourmet grocery store in Modesto. Glad my husband isn't along to witness this detour. His thoughts, "What's wrong with the cheese at King Soopers?" True, the expedient does not begin to compare with O'Brien's. Perhaps my sister is on to something. Maybe quality does matter in the small corners of life.

Deadlines, arrival times, never the strong suit for either myself or my sister. So much for picking up the keys for the rental house at 3:00 p.m. Valley traffic, nonstop trucks on the 99. My sister, ever a swift driver, is altered. She swerves off the road at one point, lulled by the audiotapes that usually rev her up.

The pain medications are slowing her down. We switch drivers, a large reparation for one who values speed. Of the two of us, I am the tortoise, the plodder, the workhorse, the marathoner. Comfortable with winding, mountain terrain, it's best that I drive this section. We traverse the tree-studded Sierra mountains, ever beautiful in spite of the brittle, dry, drought befallen the state.

Winding mountain roads—this feels like Colorado, even though I know it is Lake Tahoe. As we crest the hill, the magnificent blue of Tahoe expands before us. No, not Colorado. No body of water in

Colorado ever compares to this expanse of blue. Memories of ski trips, honeymoons, rented cabins, camping trips in the area flood back when I take in the view. Maybe coming here wasn't just about corralling the Tahoe cousins into connection. It is a beautiful location, a draw for even the Pacific Grove cousins. Any place outside of Merced, a call for my sister. I wonder how much of her cancer comes from living in the valley, agricultural pesticides, sprays, and long drives to cities of culture. She has made a life there, survived by trips to civilization—San Francisco, France, Australia, Hawaii. Travel, the consolation prize, although, now I see the merits of small town living, lack of congestion, good, loyal friends. Maybe she is the victor after all.

My cousin, Mike, has missed us by five minutes at the rental house. Forty years he has not had to witness the broken time management skills of his cousins, the ones in charge of this reunion. Mike holds the family genealogy suitcase, inherited from his father, my godfather, who, without the aid of computers, sat hours in the Stanford library, wrote countless letters to relatives, traveled to villages in Germany, and combed church records to create our past family footprint.

Cell phone calls, back and forth, to Cousin Becky, ever the organizer, communicator, "doer" in the Neitling family. Never mind that we promised dinner tonight. We beg for an extra 60 minutes and shift into the gear so frequent and comfortable—overdrive, pedal to the metal, last minute panic mode. I reflect on how much of our lives both my sister and I have operated in this mode. My husband says we are not realistic about how long it will take to accomplish tasks. We never plan for unexpected delays, road work, fallen cakes, sick children. Instead, we underestimate time like miserly scrooges and then suffer the stress of tardiness. I think there may be a gene in the DNA makeup for this. Our Neitling cousins do not carry this gene, but the Bindel cousins are superior in over-estimating time, also. We never had to worry about being late for any of the nine Bindel weddings because we knew we were related in heart, mind, and blood. I love that my sister and Bindel cousins carry this trait. They understand and don't judge our lateness. We tolerate theirs. After all, the Bindels had nine kids in their family to get out the door on time. Our parents only had two. I am sure it drove my father into an early grave. Perhaps, my sister and I are doing the same to our husbands. They have tried in vain to reform this genetic defect and made some strides, but the damage is there, deep within the chromosomes.

Dragging in the coolers, bags, groceries up two flights of stairs I realize the downside of reserving the rental house months ago. Over-estimating the energy and capacity of my sister, the altitude is taking its toll. Not sure I could have found a one story rental house of quality in Lake Tahoe other than dingy, older log cabins. I was definite about having the reunion venue be new, upscale, large enough to force communal connection and it was that, except for the stairs. My sister moves into overdrive and her logical brain kicks in. She has always been logical, sequential in her thought processes. She thinks to turn on the oven to bake the lasagna, unearth the salad ingredients, and focus on the details of the meal. I, on the other hand, focus on organizing the counter and boxes, an unnecessary task considering our time crunch. My pathology and coping mechanisms, tidiness, has its shadow side. I know this about myself, recognize the anxiety. Finally, I find the placemats and accomplish a useful necessary task to get the meal on the table before the cousins arrive.

Friday night is the smaller reunion, with part of the Neitling cousins. The Bindel girl cousins call to say they will be much later than expected, perhaps midnight, and would we leave the door unlocked. Their brother, Bill, his wife Donna, and their three large Australian shepherds, do attend the Friday night fete. No matter that I specifically said, "No dogs allowed." The dogs sat in their truck, barked, and then my sister insisted we bring the dogs in. They are sweet, well behaved animals, better behaved than any of our dogs or children ever thought of being. I feel good about the decision to risk eviction from the rental house. The dogs are the children Bill's wife, Donna, never had, and my sister and I empathize with this connection. Our dogs have always been at the top of the family chain. Ill-behaved and flawed, we loved them unconditionally, perhaps more than our human relatives. My cousin, Bill, appears to have skipped the lateness gene. He looks so much like his father, Gil, my uncle. The Bindel girls are through and through related to us. They are late, GPS dependent, dog loving, kind, compassionate women. So much of what our mothers valued, these proud German/French women from tiny little Sublimity, Oregon, has transferred to their daughters, my sister, my cousins, me.

The Neitling cousins and their mom, Phillis, my only living aunt (by marriage, not DNA) arrive bringing gifts. I am touched that they cared enough to show this appreciation, a joint gift from the girl Neitling cousins, Carrie, Becky, and Maureen, and their mom Phillis. Maureen is my sister's first godchild so she and her father are the glue that connects our families through the church. Their family lived their faith, while my sister and I skirted the perimeter of Catholicism. We did not go to parochial school. The public schools in Walnut Creek were stellar in comparison to the Catholic schools and nothing was more sacred to my mother than education. She was forced to drop out of high school before graduation, a sacrificial lamb to help her ailing mother. She vowed nothing would interrupt our education. My mother did her Catholic duty, raising us as baptized Catholics, helping us reach communion and confirmation, and attending Sunday Mass. Early on, it became obvious I was the challenge. Never one to sit still for long, my mother left me at home until age 7, when it was considered a sin not to attend Mass. I played hooky from release time Catechism and generally resented my difference from the predominant Protestant peer group. Both the Bindel and Neitling cousins were entrenched in their faith, attending parochial school, saying grace at meals, marrying in the church. My sister and I played the part, but thank our mother to this day for helping us see the other side of religion. Our mother was not really a believer and we picked up on this discrepancy.

Sitting with my cousins over the course of the reunion weekend, I am struck by how those common family values have been woven into the fabric of who we are. In spite of very different paths in life, there is the common thread of kindness, compassion, animal loving, fairness that came from our parents. The church played a role, no doubt, with guilt and sin a small stick of recrimination. It was the larger role modeling that seeped into our bones. The message that we are responsible for those less fortunate, that we do have a responsibility to help others along the way. I am thankful for this time with my cousins to see how very much alike we all are in the qualities that matter in this world.

Lock and Key

Security is something we all appreciate and sometimes feel an essential requirement in life. Locks, keys, security cameras, secret codes, passwords—all devices to insure our security.

As an owner of a mini warehouse facility, I have come to understand that there is no such thing as the indestructible lock and the magic key. Case-hardened locks can be ripped with grit, brawn, and a quality bolt cutter. An electric drill with grinding wheel functions to effortlessly melt through the very best lock on any storage unit. So much for the physical lock and key.

We have upped the ante with security cameras which record the type of movements of honest and dishonest entrants to our facility. My husband has spent countless hours positioning the cameras to maximize the views of our most vulnerable storage units. At best, we can decipher the color and make of the getaway vehicles and capture a clear image of a masked burglar and hidden license plate. Then there is the high tech security fence and gate. The gate is programmed with electronic security codes, a type of lock. The key has numerous design faults, namely the memory of a human being who has been given a secret code. Decisions, decisions, all in the name of security and providing a fool-proof lock and key for the tenants who store their life's possessions in our building.

It is true that the greater number of individuals involved in any endeavor causes a decrease in the security of that endeavor. When I reflect on the history of the women employed in the manufacture of the atomic bomb during World War II, I marvel at the security level developed with this many people. How my husband and I wish we could find these loyal, patriotic souls today and give them jobs at Re-Max, our property management company.

The real estate agents are charged with distributing the secret gate codes, recording the names of prospective tenants, and drawing up a rental lease for paying storage unit clients. This seems simple enough on the surface, but there are several steps where the lock and key are lost. Recording the codes, recording the name of the code's owner, recording the unit number, and completing a lease are several places where the key to the lock can be lost or misplaced.

The "looky-loos" are given a onetime secret code, which my husband has learned to delete on a regular basis. Otherwise, this key is floating out among the real estate agents and the general public with liability for misuse. Once a tenant vacates the unit, the code needs to be erased so that the former tenant cannot return and shop for interesting items in other people's units. With all these cyber keys and locks floating around, another lock and key system was needed, knowledge of the time and date any secret code user is entering the storage facility. With this knowledge, we know which code has been utilized on any given day. If the tenant has not paid, we can change his key, his secret code. If the entrant has criminal intentions, as evidenced by the security camera capturing their burglary effort, we can see who has entered at any given day and moment in time. Although we cannot see the masked burglar, we do know which key or secret code they used.

After thirty-three years as mini storage owners, we understand how all locks have keys that can be removed, damaged, breeched, and circumvented. Security is an illusion. Hide your valuables under the bed and hope for the best.

We write to taste life twice,
in the moment and in retrospect.

Anais Nin

Cara Koch

Born in the Black Hills of South Dakota, Cara graduated from South Dakota State University with a major in Home Economics, specializing in child development and family relationships. She began her 40 year career in the field of early childhood in Denver, Colorado, during the first year of the Head Start program. She later obtained her Master's degree in childcare administration from Wheelock College in Boston. Following retirement, she returned to school for a doctorate in children's (innate) spirituality from United Theological Seminary in Dayton, Ohio. Cara and her husband, Harry Wrede, who is retired from the US Air Force, have lived for many years in Colorado Springs. She is currently AAUW Public Policy Director for the Colorado Springs Branch.

Coming of Age in the Sixties

It was in 1966, the first year of the Head Start Program, when I first met Asa, the man I would later marry. Fresh out of college, I was the newly hired Head Start teacher at a center located in the heart of Denver's black ghetto; he was the parent counselor. A tall, good-looking black man with strong, broad shoulders, he always wore a crisp white shirt and tie paired with carefully creased dress pants. Asa reminded me of pictures of civil rights workers frequently featured in newspaper articles about Martin Luther King.

One morning after our initial meeting, I looked up to see Asa coming into the center holding the hand of four year old Stacey, who walked shyly beside him. Her eyes glanced up at him for reassurance as they entered the room. An unusual little girl who withdrew from the other children, Stacey often twirled around the classroom in circles or sat rocking back and forth in a world of her own. Staff members noted the way she pulled back in fear any time a man approached her in the classroom. Except for Asa. Seeing him bend down to whisper in her ear that morning, I felt my heart warm. The tension in her thin little body seemed to melt in response as his hand gently touched her back. *This is the kind of father I want for my children*, I found myself thinking.

Following my college graduation in January of 1966, I had driven to Denver in my shiny, newly-refurbished '59 Oldsmobile. With my new degree, I was thrilled to be in pursuit of a career in the field I loved. I was jumping into my future with both feet: *Denver, here I come!*

Growing up in Custer, in the Black Hills of South Dakota, left me hungry to experience the world beyond. Surrounded by a pine forest, we kids had the perfect summer activity: packing a picnic lunch with friends for a hike to the Custer sign at the top of a rock outcropping that overlooked our town. In winter we walked the train tracks to a lake for ice skating. Everything sprang to life during the three months of peak tourist season when the 32 motels in town all had no vacancy signs. High school kids were needed to work in the restaurants and filling stations, so my girlfriends and I waited tables while the boys usually pumped gas to earn spending money and save for college.

Custer was a place where hard work ranked high in the scheme of things. Though some people had more financial assets than others, anyone who worked hard was respected. The American ideal of equality that we learned about in grade school history class seemed pretty much a reality, and my friends and I all assumed this was true everywhere—everywhere, that is, except in the South with blacks. The stories of slavery, the KKK, and segregation sounded abominable to us—like stories from a foreign country. We believed that class distinction everywhere else in the US was a thing of the past, left behind in Europe when the Revolutionary War was won. Details, such as the fact that "we the people" actually meant "white male property owners only" when the Constitution was first written, were not stressed in my 1950's history classes.

Minorities were seldom seen in Custer. Native Americans lived mostly on the reservations miles away, though we occasionally played some of their basketball teams in high school—and usually got pretty badly beaten. Only three or four mixed race families (Native American and white) lived in town and had children in public school. These kids were usually strong athletes, and were well-liked by the rest of us. There was little racial distinction—that is, until we were old enough to date. By the second half of high school, interracial dating was either discouraged or forbidden by parents, and although all my friends and I felt this limit to be unjust, we generally did not challenge it.

My friends' mothers were homemakers who sometimes helped their fathers run small businesses such as a gas station, grocery store, car dealership, bar, lumber mill, or a clothing store. By the time I was in school my father had established a cabinet making and home building/remodeling business. Although my mother had attended college and taught school until I was born, she stayed home to raise me and my brother until we were in high school.

Driving west across the wide open plains of Wyoming to Cheyenne, then heading south to Denver, the employment possibilities I hoped to discover trickled through my mind.

After student teaching preschool in the lab school at SDSU, I could easily picture myself as a teacher in Head Start. Part of the War on Poverty, the vision for Head Start was that it would eradicate poverty. I felt a surge of excitement as I pictured myself working with children who would otherwise be behind when they started school. I was confident that, by providing a crucial head start in all the basics a child needs for intellectual, physical, social and emotional development, I could play a small part in transforming our country into The Great Society. My excitement was fueled by the reports of my favorite professor, who had gone to Washington DC the year before to help develop the National Head Start guidelines.

Up to now I had not strayed much beyond the borders of my Midwestern upbringing, so it never even occurred to me that Head Start children in Denver might have skin color different from my own.

Teaching in this setting opened up a new world of learning for me. As the four-year-olds came pouring in the door on my first morning, we had their name tags ready—a matter of survival for a new teacher in a sea of 40 little brown faces. Complicating this was the fact that all those faces looked just alike. But by the end of the day I was able to see past their complexion and recognized individual faces as easily as I had back in my college lab school.

It was amazing to discover how creatively children growing up in the dismal environment of a city ghetto responded to whatever activities we improvised. One of my favorite memories is seeing the children seated around the table as they rhythmically kneaded their play dough and spontaneously broke into song: "Ah,a-a-men, ah,a-,a-men, ah-amen, amen , amen!"

In order to acquaint me with Denver's black community, Asa impressed me with his knowledge as he pointed out the original boundaries of the black community that segregated the black ghetto from the more affluent parts of town.

He pointed out how boundaries later expanded to the more affluent Colorado Boulevard, and later even further to Park Hill, a charming residential neighborhood that was in the process of becoming integrated. Here were stately homes on beautiful tree-lined boulevards, with attractive bungalows and front porches lining the side streets between the boulevards. The northern part of Park Hill was mostly black, while the blocks going south graduated from mixed to totally white.

"Park Hill has recently experienced 'white flight'," Asa explained, "with many whites moving out in order to escape the changing complexion of the neighborhood. But there is a strong coalition of others who see an opportunity for Park Hill to become a model integrated neighborhood. Right now most of the whites left are here by choice, and Park Hill has achieved national recognition as a successfully integrated neighborhood."

When Asa and I married and bought our Park Hill home a couple of years later in 1968, we were the first family to integrate our block.

As Asa educated me about the black experience in Denver and America, I was swept away by the eloquence and passion with which he told his own story; with his hopeful attitude regarding the civil rights movement; and with the charm and charisma he displayed in working with families in the Head Start community. Such a contrast to the men I had known from South Dakota! They usually spoke in short sentences peppered with slang and spent most of their time working on cars or hunting, seldom expressing feelings except with profanity. Of course there were some smart engineer types, but for the most part the engineers communicated better with slide rules than other people.

Asa seemed strong, yet sensitive, and articulate—so different from my father, whom I judged to be a weak, submissive man who got along by pleasing others and being run by my mother. Dad was a good provider for our family, though he had only an 8th grade education. Perhaps it was due to the difference in my parents' education—she had graduated from Normal School and had an intellectual bent—that he deferred to her. He was a self-taught but skilled cabinet maker and carpenter who contracted to build and remodel homes.

"Jim, it's time for your bath now," she would say to him every evening, in the infantilizing tone of a mother talking to a small child. He always complied. Actually, they each had their weaknesses for which the other compensated. My mother's anxiety about finances exaggerated her sense of financial dependence on my father. Although he was a good, steady provider, nothing could compensate for the anxiety she felt as a result of her father's deserting his family during the depression when he couldn't find work. She had to be in charge.

I later came to feel considerable shame about my erroneous judgment of my father as weak. Through the skewed lens of my parents' relationship, Asa appeared to me to be a strong, sensitive, charismatic man who was a leader of others—someone who would be my knowledgeable, sensitive protector in the new, unfamiliar world I was entering.

Through his stories of growing up in Jefferson, Texas, a small town near the Louisiana border in the heart of the segregated South, I soon learned how different his background was from mine. His father was a restaurant cook who took great pride in supporting his family of two sons and three daughters, a rarity among black families of the time. Most black men could not support their families.

"Daddy never did let Mama do any hard work when I was a baby," Asa told me with pride. "He'd come home after work and scrub the floors himself so she wouldn't have to. One time he came home with a new tricycle for me, before I could even walk."

The life he described was not easy, however. They often had to move overnight when his father found it necessary to leave town for some unexplained reason.

"My father had a lot of anger in him," Asa explained, leading up to a story about the time a white customer yelled at him in the restaurant.

"Hey, Nigger! My coffee's cold! Take this back and bring me some *hot* coffee!"

"Yassir, yassir," replied his father, who took the cup back to the kitchen and placed it upside down on the hot stovetop before refilling it and returning it to the unsuspecting customer.

"Here's your coffee for you, Sir. Is it hot enough, Sir?" The man touched his lips to the cup—and then cried out in pain.

I suspect it was situations like this that caused the middle-of-the-night moves.

This lifestyle for Asa's family came to an abrupt halt when Asa was about twelve. His father developed a severe cough and was diagnosed with throat cancer. Since no one would hire a cook who coughed so much in the kitchen, he could no longer get a job. Asa's mother was forced to go to work as a domestic, cooking for a white family in town.

"She didn't have to do any housecleaning or anything like that, though," Asa said proudly. There was other help to do that."

The irony was his father lived for 13 more years without any cancer treatment. Asa figured he never did have cancer, but to my knowledge he never worked again.

Asa told me he had not done well in school. The quality of segregated schools in Jefferson was comparable to the quality of medical care for blacks, and he soon found himself kicked out of the house by his father.

"You ain't learnin' nothin' in school no-how, Boy. You need to learn to make it on your own."

He headed for Dallas to live with a cousin, and soon found himself caught up in a gang.

"I had no way to protect myself, so I found an old chain that I carried when I went out," he told me. "One night some gang members tried to corner me, but I just swung that chain real hard at them, and got away. Later they found me and told me they wanted me to join their gang. I didn't feel like I had much choice."

This was a part of Asa's story that was hard for me to relate to. Gangs were foreign to me, and he did not seem to be anything like someone who would have been in a gang.

"The military was my way out of Dallas," he told me. "I got lucky. After a short time as a private in the Army, I taught myself to play a saxophone. I hated doing the grunt work I had to do as a regular soldier, so I wanted to join the Army band. I made it through the try-outs, and ended up getting to travel all over Europe with other musicians, giving concerts. I loved that life, and I loved being in Germany. I was called *Schwartz* American there—*Schwartz* is German for "black"—and it wasn't derogatory. I found out how it felt to be equal."

"I sent money back home the whole time I was overseas," Asa told me. "My family had moved in with Big Mama while I was gone." Big Mama was Asa's mother's mother, a light skinned woman of mixed ancestry—probably indigenous Indian and white—who was the family matriarch.

"Big Mama owned her own house, and I wanted them to fix it up. It didn't turn out that way, though. When I got home it was as run down as when I left. My father had gambled away all the money , and nobody—not a single one of them—told me. All that money, gone to waste."

Asa eventually confided that he had gotten in a fist fight with his father over his gambling away of the money. After that he left home for good, following his sister to Denver.

"Though I loved being a musician in Germany, I knew I could not continue that life style in the US. A black musician's life here in the States is one of doping and drinking. I didn't want that, so I sold my saxophone and never played again."

Asa also told me that when his father died in 1963 he went back to Texas for the funeral, but was still so angry with him he could not bring himself to attend the service.

It was little more than a year after I came to Denver when Asa and I decided we wanted to be married. Climbing into my new Chevy Impala, he in his white shirt and tie, and me in my Easter suit, we made the day's drive to South Dakota so Asa could ask my father for my hand in marriage. Following the plan he proposed, Asa drove me to my parents' home and dropped me off. My anxiety level dropped a notch when they greeted us both warmly before he left to drive the 30 miles back across the Wyoming state line. He was to spend the night in a motel in a little Wyoming town by the name of New Castle. As we drove through New Castle on our way to Custer, Aaron flagged down a local policeman.

"Sir, I have never been to Wyoming before, so I do not know how people here feel about blacks," he explained. "I am driving Cara here to see her parents in Custer, and then I will come back here to stay at the Blue Bird Motel overnight. I just want to let you know where I will be in case there are any problems."

"Oh, I don't think you have nothin' to worry about, "he drawled in his western twang. "We don't have no trouble with blacks around these parts 'cause none of 'em live here. But I will drive by to keep an eye on things, jus' the same. Thanks for checkin' in with me," the officer said before pulling away in his cruiser.

"To make sure the cops are with me, not against me," was Asa's explanation for what had just transpired.

Pleased that Asa wanted to ask my father for my hand, I was not too sure about how it would turn out. My mother had expressed concern for some time about my having a relationship with a black man, but put most of the reason on my father. "He is likely to disown you if you keep pursuing this," she warned. Since there had been no opportunity for the issue of race to come up in our family before this, I had no first-hand knowledge of what to expect from my father. The only family history I had ever heard regarding blacks was the story about the time my Grandfather—my father's father—was escorting a shipment of cattle on the train from Wyoming to Chicago when my father was a child. He had physically defended a black man on the train.

The way Asa handled things next amazed me. He somehow arranged for my Dad and the two of us to be in the car without my mother present.

"Jim, I have something important to ask you," he said as my father drove down the road. "I want to ask your permission to marry Cara."

Shirlea Griswold

Having lived everywhere and nowhere in an R.V. for 11years, I finally came to light in Colorado Springs. It is a delight every day with its natural beauty, friends and family. Devouring anything with words and/or pictures takes me to the past, present and future. Wheels and wings have been adventures to different cultures near and far. They all feed the gypsy, nerd, adventurer and rebel in me. There is a need to create, learn and explore in different mediums from computer and pen to sparkly colorful beads and malleable clay and who knows what else keeps my right brain energized while dusting and weeding has my left brain somewhat grounded.

I can be found puttering in my craft room, playing on the computer, enjoying different groups, traveling hither and yon, watching aname or reading sprawled in a chair.

Choices

Have you thought about what you would change in your life and how it would change the world? Change your life change the world.

I have – many times. That is thought about what I would change in my past. Realizing the problems, the mistakes, and each and every choice have made me who I am today. If somehow they were taken away or changed not only would my life be different so would of everyone around me.

The next generation constantly amazes me – including my children. They are different than I would have planned their life for them. They are interesting and unique and much better than my wonderful plans would have been.

Remember if a butterfly dies in South America the world changes. The physicists now believe that the earth or Gaia is a complicated set of systems that work together. Each and every person on the earth somehow is interconnected with these multiple systems. Yes we do screw it up often. How else explain that new ideas or thoughts seem to become inventions and creations in several places in the world at almost the same time. This has been called the hundredth monkey.

If I were to change anything I would change the time I was born – bring it forward 50 years so I could be a part of the information – digital – graphics age. Again that would change everything for many people. Why the information age? Because so much can be done creatively on the computer. This is evident every time I go to the movies. But then 3D printing is the next big creative step. Who knows when the "best" time for creativity would be?

The classic painters made their own paint or an assistant did. Their colors are extraordinary. The Egyptians' jewelry has never been equaled. The South American Incas made buildings that were so well built they still stand the test of time. You cannot get a tool of any kind in between the huge blocks they built with. Even with our amazing tools and instruments we cannot duplicate any of these extraordinary accomplishments.

So for my family and friends I will still vote for leaving my life exactly as it was and is.

Puddles

There were occasional dimly lit carriage lamps along the dark gravel road. The sky was studded with stars that night.

There had been a drought for several months. Everything was dry, the trees were drooping, plants were almost nonexistent, even the few flowers were turning peculiar colors and of course the roadway itself. Every step I took small clouds of brown dust coated every surface it touched with its grime.

Upon turning a corner the street was wet in a strange way. It didn't resemble any rain I had ever seen. If there had been more light the pattern would have been more comprehensible. What I saw was incomprehensible.

The further I walked the closer together the puddles were. They were different colors near the lamps. They were gray and opaque further away in the starlight and moonlight.

After rambling along for a block wondering what had made these puddles fascinating I saw someone walking a few yards ahead of me who wore a long black trench coat. As I slowly gained it seemed it was raining around this person. He held an umbrella overhead which had blue blinking stars on it. Oh!! There was a flash of lightning above him now and then too!

Getting ever closer it became clear it was neither a man nor a woman. Only a coat, the unusual umbrella and a pair of black wellies moved down the road together enjoying their personal storm. Sometimes skipping or dancing, twirling, wiggling and shaking. When he wiggled and shook he splattered water all around creating puddles of wonder.

Suddenly, whatever this was, realized I was behind it and not very far by then. Poof! It disappeared. It left me shivering alone on a dark lonely solitary night with dimly lit carriage lamps here and there along a dark gravel road.

The Complexion Disaster

She grimaced at the message on her computer screen. It was pretty clear the opportunity had run its course. While she had been gone to the mall for lunch the lab had finished the last experiments on skin pigmentation. The research had come up with nothing.

Anita, it was a bust all around. She was definitely in trouble. The drugs, the herbs, and who knows what else she had been fed and taken over the last two weeks hadn't worked. She felt she had run out of options.

Remembering the morning three weeks ago she had looked in the mirror and saw the horrible change. Once again she cringed and slumped in discouragement.

If the scientist and innovators didn't come up with something, anything quickly that worked, her beautiful light emerald green complexion would be stuck with very fine lines of neon purple. Where the purple had come from she didn't know or care just so it would go away and leave her with her perfectly beautiful light emerald skin.

How could she stand it if the condition were forever?

Chris Edgar

Most people have wishes about wanting to live in a different time. They long for the past or wish for the future. I, Chris Edgar, have been very fortunate to live in a time in history that was just right for me. With a solid upbringing in a small community (an island outside Stockholm, Sweden), where my parents introduced me to the world around me through literature, history and debate. Through poetry and prose I became curious about the globe, its people and nature's many wonders.

As a global nomad, I have explored and participated. I have lived in two societies (the latter being my adopted home in the foothills of the Colorado Rockies). The future makes me excited. Every morning means new opportunities, new possibilities.

You cannot walk alone. I am grateful to family and friends for wanting to share my journey. It is my hope that you, the readers, enjoy it as well.

Dedicated to my son, James W. Edgar

Peace

Did it ever happen before? Silence in the neighborhood
Mother's Day, 1990 and I was there to savor the moment.

Walking barefooted. Wet grass. Early morning
Birds chirping, Japanese apple tree
Red flowers covering every inch of every branch
Proud tulips turning their heads toward the sun.

Tiny aspen leaves, pale green whispering good morning to the world.
P.J., our faithful Shih Tzu, checking out his domain, our garden.

No wind. No planes circling in the air.
No cars starting up. No lawn mowers. No human voice,
Only birds, the sun and the blue sky,
Acting as a backdrop for the mountain range.

In a vase downstairs I found
A red rose from my child,
The young adult, still dwelling in dreamland.

It is Mother's Day

A Christmas Message

The celebration is taking place in Bethlehem at this moment...

When we were children, my sister and I listened as our parents read from the leather bound family bible, "*Och det hande sig vid den tiden att fran Kejsar Augustus utgickett pabud att hela varlden skulle skattskrivas*" - Luke2:1

We were in the living room with the Christmas tree lit up by handmade candles. You could feel the warmth and love enveloping you. Part of our tradition was to open up the door to the patio, so that we could listen to the church bells ringing from around Stockholm.

Christmas morning our family would make its way in the snow to attend services in the little whitewashed church, Lidingo kyrka. When I had to give up my Swedish citizenship, the Lutheran church kept my membership.

While I was reflecting on childhood memories, it struck me how many times I have been privileged to attend services around the world. My first thought was of arriving in London after the war and seeing St. Paul's cathedral rise among the rubble left from airstrikes during WW II. It was a sight never to be forgotten.

Next, my mind wandered to Rome, where my sister and I were together some years ago. I will never forget being in St. Peter's Basilica where a window high above the pews made you feel as if you were permitted a glimpse into Heaven.

Well, there is another place that is forever tucked into my memory bank. I was living with a family in Paris and attending la Sorbonne. One Sunday morning Madame said to me that we were all attending mass at Sacre Coeur-the white marble church in Montmartre. When I said that I was not Catholic, she told me that I was to do what they did. There I was kneeling and holding on to my rosary.

After I moved to Colorado Springs, I have attended services with and without my son, James, at the Chapel at the Air Force Academy at Easter and Prince of Peace Lutheran church during candle light services at Christmas as well as at Grace Episcopal Church when a jazz band, performed a New Orleans funeral march.

Some years back I had a friend, who loved to travel and who also had connections to Hispanic and Native American culture. During one vacation, we drove to Abiquiú, New Mexico, and she was telling me about the Penitentes and their history pertaining to Northern New Mexico and Southern Colorado. Since she knew the way, we turned up the road on the San Juan Reservation, while I listened to stories about funeral practices and alabados, or hymns, sung at the Moradas. Tucked into the hills, there is not one but two Moradas. Grey clay buildings without windows. Outside you see three wooden crosses. Georgia O'Keeffe was allowed to live in the village. Was she aware of the Moradas and the history of the Penitentes?

In 2005, we were driving north from Santa Fe Easter morning. Along the road we saw the many pilgrims making their way on foot to EI Santuario de Chimayo. When asked if I would like to join the pilgrims at the Chapel, I hesitated – feeling very much like an outsider – but in the end I agreed. Walking among the Hispanic believers, who had journeyed for days hoping for a miracle, it was a very moving experience.

Most of you know how much I respect Native American culture and beliefs. A few years ago there was a happening in the Garden of The Gods. My grandson, Christian, and 1 were there listening to a member of the Lakota Sioux saying a prayer.

It was very long and I had whispered to Christian that we needed to be quiet and respectful. When it was over Christian said, "Do you think that God understood?" Then he added, "I think that he knows many languages."

If you ever have a chance to see the Cathedral in Santa Fe and learn about Bishop Lamy, don't miss the opportunity.

Sometime in the last five years, my sister, Babbe, and I worshipped together in Storkyrkan, the enormous and gorgeous cathedral in Old Town Stockholm, a stone's throw from the Palace. I cannot describe how much I miss my sister. She left us in 2005.

The other evening I was meditating in Shove chapel at Colorado College. "Oh come let us adore him, Christ the Lord".

The world is changing. With the words of Christian, who said, "Grandma, I think that the future has already arrived".

December 24, 2008

We Shall Overcome

It seems appropriate on a day like today – the Martin Luther King holiday – that I sit down to remember some things that touched me personally since I arrived in America.

In the spring of 1961, I was invited to a National Conference in Atlantic City. I came there from West Chester State College, Pennsylvania where I had been asked to lecture and teach the students majoring in Physical Education. While at the conference, I was introduced to several professors from Tuskegee Institute, now The University of Tuskegee, Alabama. The founder: Booker T. Washington. He invited George Washington Carver of peanut fame to join his faculty.

An invitation was extended to me. Would I like to spend a few weeks teaching the students about gymnastics, my specialty?

When I accepted, I knew very little about Mr. Washington. The same goes for the plight of the blacks having to sit in the back of the bus, not being allowed to drink from the same drinking fountain as whites and much more. Nor did 1 know about the Supreme Court decision and the landmark case of Brown vs Board of Education.

Picture me on the bus going through the South. Through the windows I could see the intriguing landscape – rolling hills and dogwood trees in bloom. Spring was in the air. I was young and pleased about my new adventure. To tell the truth, I was totally unaware that I was to be the only white student on campus.

Upon arrival, I was installed in a bungalow, the guest house for non-white visitors. On the dresser was a copy of Booker T. Washington's autobiography. He was the first black to dine at the White House! Did you know? This was my introduction to the black south.

When a fellow visitor from India invited me to dinner, I accepted. We were driving toward the restaurant when we heard sirens. There were flashing lights all around us. As we pulled over, state troopers approached the car and flashed beams of light toward my face. Interracial contacts were against the law. Whatever words were exchanged, we were allowed to continue.

Once I came to Colorado Springs and started my first job at the oldest high School in town, a large portion of my students were black. I learned to appreciate their style and their good sense of humor. A few years later, a wonderful black woman, became my colleague. We used to eat at lunch counters in the neighborhood and shook off the stares from customers. We joked about integrating the neighborhood. That was the 1960s.

In the last several years, it has been my privilege to serve on several different committees in the region.

As an immigrant, who came here on a student visa, I became involved with the Pikes Peak Immigrant and Refugee Collaborative or PPIRC, working to help newcomers to Colorado Springs from other countries connect with the welcoming community. We arranged for Dialogue Circles among other activities-opportunities for people of different ethnicities to meet and talk to each other.

As a member of the Minority Overrepresentation Committee of the 4th Judicial District, I was a member of the planning committee for the first Summit on "Educating Children of Color" in 2008. The goal is to break the pipeline "From Cradle to Prison" for non-white young people. More than 450 participated. I had the honor of reading Maya Angelou's poem entitled "A Pledge to Rescue Our Youth":

> *Young women, young men of color,*
> *We add our voices to the voices of your ancestors*
> *We speak to you over ancient seas and*
> *Across impossible mountain tops.*
> *You are the best we have.*
> *You are all we have.*
> *You are what we have become.*
> *We pledge you our whole hearts from this day forward."*

A few weeks ago, 550 people attended the 2nd annual Summit on Educating Children of Color".

Today we honor Martin Luther King and his *I Have a Dream* speech.

Tomorrow, Barak Obama, the first African-American ever elected to the highest office, will put his hand on the Lincoln bible when he is sworn in as the 44th President of the United States of America.

In a speech yesterday Mr. Obama said, "Despite the enormity of the task that lies ahead I stand here today as hopeful as ever that the United States will endure, that the dream of our founders will live on in our time."

We pray for his success!

January 19, 2009

A Glimpse of my World

Trying to give you a glimpse of my world
How could you understand?

The beauty of the prairie in springtime.
Grazing antelope. Newborn foal.
Meadowlarks on fences along pastures.
Wildflowers. Indian Paintbrush.

The Sangre de Cristo range.
The Blood of Christ.
Snow-covered mountains in the morning sun.
Gold in 'thar' hills.

Thunder along the foothills.
Showers during summer afternoons.
Clear blue skies come early evening.
Blazing sunsets.

The Garden of the Gods. My sanctuary.
The trickling stream. Old homestead.
Chickadee. Bunnies. Ducks in the pond.
Being enveloped by nature.

June 18, 2003

Lani Manning

I write because I spoke an intention in the parking lot prior to attending an AAUW Colorado Springs Branch Authors' Day held at the Garden of the Gods Club. During the break for lunch, I selected a seat next to an unfamiliar woman. We introduced ourselves and soon Kathleen Visovatti shared that she participated in a writing group through her AAUW Littleton-South Metro Branch. She happened to have a dear friend from that writing group who recently moved to Colorado Springs. I left that Authors' Day with Phyllis Sperber's phone number.

I write because it's hard. Term papers, essay questions on tests, the report finalizing my internship – my mind is blank until it's not. And sometimes not is never.

I write because I thought I needed to experience writing; specifically since I might be suggesting it to others as a means to share their stories.

I write to honor the intention that placed before me Kathleen, Phyllis and the remarkable Women Who Write Beneath the Peak. Once a month, I am fearless. I arrive. I write to the prompt. I share. I may write three sentences while others write six pages. We validate and celebrate, wherever on one's journey.

I write with abiding gratitude to all.

Prompted to Begin

March

My mind has ruminated over this for many years. The wives of Vietnam War veterans have stories to tell. Unlike the generations of World War II, the Korean conflict, the Iraq and Afghanistan wars, these women (and their children) of the Vietnam era were not in the public consciousness. They were the original practitioners of "don't ask, don't tell." No one offered their veteran spouses so much as a free cup of coffee upon returning home. These women supported each other through the unpopular war, some creating their own community. How did they manage?

Women speak. That's what we do. Have these women spoken – shared their stories with each other, with their friends, with their spouses, with their children? Do they feel a need to speak? I need to listen.

April

It's April, a bit early for most to be writing a Christmas letter…but in my case, five years late. I need to reconnect. I recognize that my best intentions to write the holiday letter over Thanksgiving weekend will not be accomplished (again). Five years is a long time to be out of touch.

May Prompt: Imagination

Imagination – that which I haven't. One needs memory and imagination to write. One benefits from the ability to reconstruct events through the mind's eye and the ability to visualize that which isn't.

I've never understood those relaxation exercises. Imagine yourself on a beach…feel the sun, the breeze…smell the salt air…hear the waves, the seagulls, the palm fronds in the breeze…feel yourself relaxing, toe by toe…my mind would be blank.

But then I attended our first gathering of writers, creative writers, Women Who Write. Once again I walked into an unfamiliar place – the story of my life. I heard the word "journalist." Oh, that's my connection…ever the optimist.

August Prompt: Traditions, rituals

Oh, family rituals. Reminiscing brings smiles to most. People are anxious to share, their memories flow so freely. I recall no holiday traditions or tooth fairy rituals. I always thought it was because of my memory, or lack thereof. It turns out my siblings, with their laser-like memories, also have no recall of "family" traditions or rituals. They play Scrabble, Trivial Pursuit and even beat the Jeopardy clock. I'd simply like to recall everyone's favorite from Thanksgiving dinner and, on a grander scale, recall how the frozen turkey and canned pumpkin transformed into the feast on the table. I'm presuming there was a Thanksgiving feast.

I have to dig deep for my three Christmas memories – and they have nothing to do with maintaining the common threads of family or connecting generations. So, I ask myself, "What connects us?" What shared experiences do we reflect on when we gather? What rituals do we repeat, counting on each other to know the script, the parts we play? What makes our stomachs ache from laughter?

Our bond is moving, moving our mother. Moving when our mother's plans were far different from our father's. Since their divorce, moving our mother when she has no plan but to move. It's a strong connection. We're always there for each other. Even my father was involved in her moves after their divorce. It's what we do. It's who we are. It's how we're family. And there are times we laugh so hard our stomachs ache.

September Prompt: Alien

I've always known I was different. Not in a negative, inferior way – just different from others. In general, my peers finished college in four years on the same campuses where they began. Married or not, they worked in their fields of interest and seemed comfortable wearing titles such as teacher, dietitian, project manager, judge and librarian. Many raised children while continuing to work. Many achieved graduate degrees. They also managed to serve their communities, pursue hobbies and write their Christmas letters on time.

In 2008, Gary asked, "Has anyone suggested you might have ADD?" And so the journey began.

December Prompt: Optimism

"You're the Teflon woman." I think it's meant as a compliment. However, it was the Clinton era. Wasn't Teflon used to make a less than flattering point? Mary read my puzzled look and clarified. "You're not caught up in the drama of the bombings. You don't get involved in the interpersonal tiffs. You never ride the emotional rollercoaster – always even-keeled, an aura of calm, not only in the eye of the storm." It escaped the concern of professionals for 37 years. Someday, I shall feel the full range: the thrill of victory to the agony of defeat.

January Prompt: The Past

Although she's told me she'd dealt with the past, vague allusions to painful experiences creep into conversation. Shackled. Ball and chains prevent her from moving forward.

I've never understood fear of change. Why wouldn't one want to escape or avoid the discomfort? Seek out relief at any cost? It finally occurred to me. She had her way and I had mine.

I reflect on her life unrealized. What were her hopes and dreams? In place, a life of reaction, the sense of being trapped by circumstances that only others viewed as changeable.

When I first heard the word Alzheimer's, my sorrow was that time had run out. No longer time for her to make peace with the past and find joy in the present. No time to experience life, the life she had imagined. I grieved as if she'd died. And then we continued living.

February

"Aunty Avocado, where are you?! Are you in Co-lo-ra-do?!" his lilting voice drawing out the syllables as I envision his dancing eyes, entire body in rhythm as he speaks. His voice lifts me, much as I imagine that ad, "Calgon, take me away!" proposed to do. How blessed I am to witness his developing sense of humor.

He's my sister's son. I patiently (and silently) waited over a decade for his arrival. At one point, I thought she might forego children, as many of her generation do. And so now I wonder. How much joy can one heart hold?

March Prompt: Time

I have no sense of time. Five minutes, five hours. It can be the same experience. Does everyone feel that way?

So much to do, so little time. The "to do" lists flow from one day to the next.

Time is not my friend, but I want it to be. Is anyone comfortable with time?

Time is my enemy. Where are those time-free cultures?

Time management. Schedule the priorities. Prioritize?

The gift of time. That I can give. Time to listen, time to do for one or more.

Time passes.

Two years in the beginning from birth to two, then two to four. A time of growth, of miracles.

Two years in decline, then two more. How many more unmetered days marked by loss? It's expected, but strikes by surprise. It's expected, but always arrives with one feeling unprepared.

April Prompt: Memory and the senses

Lately, these questions arise: "Do you have brothers and sisters?" and "Where do they live?" in the context of how are they involved in the care of our mother? I explain. They've disengaged. They have memories and I don't. That explanation never quite suffices.

It's not exactly the lack of memory that allows me to jump back in. It's the absence of that visceral connection, that autonomic response triggered in my siblings when in contact with our mother. It's ironic that propensity is reflected in many of her interactions. My siblings have disengaged as she's often disengaged from life.

July: Steve Keating, Where Are You?

Do you recall that August day in 1970? It was my first week of high school, a new school in an unfamiliar country. You were leaning against the lockers in front of geometry class with a group of friends. You knew everyone, even me.

It was that day you introduced me to him, the one in the striped, button-down shirt and blue jeans. Later I learned he favored Gant shirts and Levis, the jeans an act of rebellion. But that's a story for another time. I was fourteen and captivated. He, with the steel trap memory, doesn't recall that day.

The school year unfolded. He asked my best friend, Kathy, to an athletic banquet. She accepted. They dated through the following school year. He treated me as one of the guys. In my naiveté I had no clue his best friend, Bill, had a crush on me....

August Prompt: Brother, sister

God gave us family so we could learn to love those we wouldn't choose to otherwise.

My Band of Sisters

Ursula, Monica, Kelly, Kate, Connie, myself and one who never appeared. Six women drawn together by time. We were all available on Saturday mornings. Only the day of the week gathering us as the tasseled purse string of a silk pouch.

What were our expectations? What were my expectations? This question was asked, "What do you hope to get out of this group?" I shared, "I've lived my life on an island, surrounded by the sea. You are all on a ship passing by. I will step off my island to join you. Can I trust you on this journey? We shall see."

March Prompt: Underdog

The Kim Sisters

Sylvia was the eldest. She was a sensitive child, traumatized by the sound of planes flying overhead on Pearl Harbor Day, her gas mask leaking during an air raid drill, and the screams of her sister protesting bath time.

Sylvia was a rebel. She argued constantly with her Korean-born mother. She preferred short, permed hair, wearing cut-offs to the library and maintained a life-long abhorrence for the color pink. Pink was her mother's favorite color.

Sylvia loved books. The library was her sanctuary. She dreamed of escape, leaving the island for the mainland and beyond.

Cynthia was an exceptional child. Born at home, as was typical of the time, she most likely suffered anoxia at birth. For years, Cynthia and her family were stigmatized with the mislabel "mongoloid". Later, it was determined to be cerebral palsy. Regardless of diagnosis, it was her mother's cross to bear....

May Prompt: Thoughts to ponder…and inspire?

Regret or Rejoice

It's been six years since Gary asked the ADD question. I never imagined my "differences" had a label. Apparently I was a master of compensation. Being acutely aware of situations where I was less than effective, I had engineered my life to avoid failure and ensure success. I suspect menopause was the straw that broke the camel's back. Could I be less "different" and more efficient? I read that ADD symptoms could be related to insufficient dopamine. I was optimistic, open to change.

A neuro-psych evaluation confirmed inattentive ADD. I tried eleven ADD meds individually titrated and in numerous combinations resulting in no significant benefit. The greatest disappointment was my lack of response to pharmaceutical grade meth. My one chance in life to get high legally…nothing!

A sleep study ruled out narcolepsy. The results did suggest circadian rhythm disorder, sleep deprivation, psychoactive drug use or depression. However, I literally slept like a log. Seven sleep-enhancing meds later it was time to move on.

I consumed every ADD book, webinar and workshop I thought might apply to me. Exercise, fish oil, CHADD meetings; the practice of mindfulness became routine. The symptoms persisted.

I finally accepted ADD medication wasn't the panacea I hoped for. After medication management, the next steps in ADD treatment are typically therapy and coaching. I sought an ADD coach. She tried. I tried. I was un-coachable, un-supervisable, and I later added un-motivatable. On to therapy….

Today I live in gratitude. It's only my brain – not a life-threatening disease. It could be so much worse.

June Prompt: Unnerving or disconcerting

Turn left on Dale, pass the dancers, left into the parking lot. Seek the shade and park. I enter the coolness of the Fine Arts Center (FAC), pause and briskly walk left. Determined, I pass beneath Chihuly. I feel enveloped. Not unlike iSpace, the FAC is a refuge, sanctuary from life "out there." A place I have to tear myself away from each time I visit.

Like weaving. My looms yet undressed from 1998. I don't weave because I can't stop. And when I do stop, I can't breathe. And so I don't start. I wonder, what do other people do?

August Prompt: What man has made, would woman do it differently?

What compels man to change the visual landscape, to create structures of enormous proportions, whether under pretense of religion or energy?

November Prompt: Mystery

David Chinkook Ro, my Grandpa David. He died when I was ten or eleven. We were living on Guam and no one from our immediate family attended his funeral in Hawaii. Not even my mother who spoke fondly, though rarely, of her father.

Grandpa David, the adventurer. He learned English from the Catholic missionaries in Korea. In his teens he sold the family cow, lied about his age to pose as an uncle's son and left his step-mother for America. Did he steal the cow? Was she evil? What happened to his mother? What about his father? How old was he at the time and what age did he assume? Who was this uncle, never referred to again in family lore?

At some point, Grandpa David arrived in Los Angeles. I have his diploma from the University of Southern California High School.

My father says he was a gentleman. I don't recall my father speaking of anyone else in quite that way....

December: Writing poetry

Gluten-free flour
needs xanthan gum
or guar gum
to bind
or suspend
ingredients.
Should I have stayed
one more year
for high school
chemistry?

Chemistry – oh, no!
The periodic table
was my downfall.
But now I understand.
So were the fifty states
and their capitals.
In fourth grade
the pattern emerges.
Eventually,
so does my humor.
There are three things
I do remember –
I have two children,
I know their birthdays,
I recall where

I last left them.
Anything else
can be looked up.

January Prompt: Key, lock

The Key to My Heart
Not gifts, not words
Nor time or touch
Just change my oil
I'll love you much

What's Key?
Today I am grateful
for my grandparents
and great-grandparents
who fled Korea.
One would expect
for political freedom
and economic opportunity.
It was simply too damn cold.

February Prompt: Strongest memory of your past

My sister was ten when she first stayed to live with us. Only ten, with a suitcase of clothes suitable for a Thanksgiving visit to Missouri, which it was intended to be. No specifics or even a conversation. Our mother left and the next day I was investigating elementary schools.

April Prompt: Wisdom and insight

When I was seventeen, I remember thinking I can't wait to be old and wise. Was this an odd thought to have while waiting to have one's wisdom teeth pulled?

When my grandfather was in his nineties my father brought him to visit our family in Castle Rock. After days of American cooking, my father knew Grandpa would enjoy a Japanese meal. As we walked through the door of the local Japanese restaurant, the proprietor and staff rushed to greet us. They bowed before Grandpa, oblivious that five of us accompanied him. They spoke in Japanese, what I imagined to be words of welcome. He was escorted to a table, leaving the rest of our family to trail behind. They asked us his age, as if speaking to him directly would be impolite. Grandpa was brought servings of food beyond that which we ordered. His presence was clearly an honor. I had only heard or read about the Japanese revering their elders. This was my first experience observing its public expression toward a stranger.

May Prompt: Visualization
Two Sides of Eighty

A tall, fit man. White lab coat, deep black jeans and always cowboy boots. E-pen in hand, navigating the laptop with confidence and precision, he taps the keyboard with his two index fingers. Men of his generation didn't learn to type. Methodically, he reads each section of the online form and follows up with questions. Sometimes he forgets to face her when he speaks. He turns and repeats the question. Patiently, he waits for her response.

She leans forward, as if to reveal a confidence. I'm sitting behind her and envision her eyes lighting up as she smiles. She may answer his question or share from the prepared agenda in her mind, "Is it true you take your staff dancing?" Occasionally she's silent while processing his questions. I feel her puzzled look. Is it the question or the answer I wonder? I wait. Only then do I respond, imagining myself a Bunraku puppet.

June Prompt: If it were up to me, I would be...

One who prepares every recipe clipped from the newspaper...at least once. When those file folders and boxes have been winnowed down, I would proceed through my collection of cookbooks. I have promised myself not to acquire one more cookbook 'til I've done so.

I would write notes to everyone who somehow touches me throughout the day. This doesn't include thank you notes, birthday cards and other Hallmark days of remembrance which I aspire to accomplish as well.

I would call simply to inquire, "How are you? What's happening?" and truly have the time to listen.

As I glance up, a hummingbird catches my eye. Miles beyond, a plane passes over. If it were up to me, would I be the plane or the hummingbird?

Rosemary Scheuering

Rosemary Scheuering has lived most of her life in Colorado, making and teaching art and English. She has resided in Manitou Springs for nineteen years, after living many years in Boulder, Colorado, and in the Denver area.

Scheuering's natural inclination in creating art and writing has always been to portray her love of landscape and nature and interpret its changing patterns. Scheuering has exhibited her visual works nationally and locally in the Colorado Springs area. In Colorado Springs, she has taught Art Appreciation at Pikes Peak Community College.

Scheuering's writing has often been in the form of curriculum writing for her school district, and for presentations she has made at the national and state level. She also wrote a chapter for art instruction in *Multicultural Art Worlds*.

Since retirement, she has produced a small volume of her paintings and thoughts in *Painted Gems of the Rockies*.

Vignettes from My Mountain Perch

Residing at 6500 feet above Manitou Springs, and below Pikes Peak which looms over 14,000 feet, I have enjoyed some good and somewhat scary experiences.

In these few recollections, I have offered some memories of my years in this special place.

The Peak

We live below it.

In our everyday world, Pikes Peak rises above us to a soaring height and spreads out its mass over many miles.

Creating its own weather, it embroils itself in rain, snow, blizzards, clouds, without concern for what we do 8,000 feet below.

At certain times, it blocks wind, snow and rain from reaching us below.

The morning sun blazes on its magnitude from the east. By late afternoon, the Peak creates a shadow on the hills below causing a cool and early evening.

Going around the city on errands and appointments, one turns and is surprised with a glorious view at any time of the day.

There are three ways to ascend the Peak: walking up and up, taking a cog railway, or driving a cliff hanging road.

The path up starts from juniper and pinon hills singing with scrub jays and chickadees and providing a protected haven for deer. The earth is colored red in this lower zone, part of a bygone age of sedimentary seas.

As one rises into the montane zone, the trees become ponderosa, with their long and hardy needles. Here the black bear thrives along with the elusive mountain lions.

There are numerous trails at this level with folks young and old testing their prowess. Here the historic Utes found a trail to their homes and hunting grounds.

As the altitude rises, firs are the prominent tree along with groves of the spreading quaking aspen. As the path becomes more vertical, there are but few trails and one auto road. Spreading out from the main highway are some side roads going to a "real" North Pole. Also, along the paved highway are reservoirs holding water for the cities below. Among these reservoirs in the enveloping hills, humankind picnics, fishes, walks, or just admires the view.

The road to the summit becomes a knife edge, and often has to be closed in winter. The summit, whether by trail, car, or cog offers 360 degree views and homage to the lady who wrote "America, the Beautiful" after being inspired by her trip.

The Peak is our guardian, our resource, our inspiration, and our challenge.

They Have Returned!

They are back!

Each spring we look forward to their arrival.

We scan the skies and watch our feeders, and listen for their song.

Some come in March like the Sandhill cranes, so beloved that they have a festival in Monte Vista, Colorado.

Some come also in April, passing over Dinosaur Ridge near Red Rocks in Denver. Watching parties scan the sky each day to count the hawks and eagles that pass over the ridge.

Everyone tunes their ears in April as the hummingbirds arrive around April 15, when bird lovers should have their sugar/water feeders out for their arrival, sometimes in snow.

At my bird sanctuary it is May 9 that I anticipate. It was my father's birthday also. Who arrives? Well, the beloved black-headed grosbeak. The colorful orange and black males arrive first, gobbling at the feeders after their long journey from Mexico.

In spite of fierce lightning storms and hail and snow the previous night, three handsome bright orange and black males were there at 10 a.m. on May 9 this year, their chosen day of return.

These colorful chaps with large beaks are exceedingly hungry and are still there past noon feeding on the suet feeders and black oiled sunflower seeds. They rather take over the smaller birds like the nuthatches and chickadees, but are willing to share somewhat in spite of their ravenous appetite.

Three days later, the girls arrive in their brown and beige streaked attire. They are also hungry. They sit at the feeders all day, recovering from their journey.

A few days later, a gorgeous western tanager arrives. He is much shyer, but stands out with his black, red and yellow raiment.

He cautiously checks out how to approach the feeder. On occasion, the female grosbeak pecks him away from the feeder. And I believe that he isn't too afraid as he was there last evening accompanied by another handsome buddy.

The days are now filled with lilting song and melodious chirps until Labor Day.

The Year of the Big Black Bear

On my mountain perch below Pikes Peak, bears sometimes come.

I know they are there because when they come up on the deck, they stomp very loudly.

They don't come often. Last year I didn't see any.

One time many years ago, a mother came with her cub. She pushed him up the pinon tree next to the deck. He wasn't moving fast enough and she gave him a big paw wallop.

I have had juvenile bears that really don't know what is going on. They rather sit and ponder at the highly rigged bird feeders.

However, one time when I was gone and before I knew how to hang my feeders high above the lower deck, I awoke one morning to a missing hummingbird feeder and a damaged deck board.

I knew it was the bear because he left a big bear claw on the side of the deck. It is still there.

But, after the big fire, HE came. The sturdy metal feeders were hung at least ten feet above the ground.

That was the night I heard a REALLY BIG BEAR. He had managed to pull down the big high feeder and was having a big snack. He lolled around for at least an hour. Then, he took a few drinks from a plant saucer, and finally faded into the darkness.

I felt better after he left because he could easily have sauntered right into my windows with his massive bulk.

The Fire

One year the rains did not come again. There had been several dry years in the area. Then someone in the forest above Colorado Springs started a fire. The person has never been discovered.

At first, it was thought just to be a small fire high up on the trail. But the fire persisted. Then the winds came and the fire rose into an angry storm.

Within a day, it was seen from everywhere. Warnings were sent out to prepare to evacuate.

I started to gather my important papers, medicines, a few clothes and a suitcase.

The storm became worse as the night came on. As I prepared to go to bed, I looked out my large stairway window. On the top of a not too distant hill, the scene was that of the edge of a volcano cauldron, vivid flames of red and gold.

It was hard to get to sleep. In the night, my neighbor called and said we should start to get ready to go. I packed several boxes, and a suitcase in the car. Soon the doorbell rang. The police officer was telling me that I should leave right now. And so, within a few minutes, I left the house, down the hill. I exchanged a few words with my neighbor about where I was going to go to spend the night. They were on their way also.

Everyone was ordered to leave the town in sections. The move through the town was orderly and quiet.

It took a while to find my friend's house in the dark. Trying to remain calm, we passed the night. Although I was allowed to go back home the next evening, I stayed with my friend two more nights. That third night became the evening when the fire went on a rampage north of my house with a devastating cloud of smoke and fire that destroyed a great portion of the north part of Colorado Springs. Two people died.

Many acquaintances lost their homes in that fire. Some have rebuilt. Some have gone to a different part of the city. And they still have horrible dreams. One does not forget.

Rain or Fire

Raining again..............bundles of rain in the last couple of weeks.

Puddles and accidents.....helping make potholes deeper.

Big rains, then little constant rains..............days of rain................

Not usual for this dry desert climate....but appreciated......yet a worry as there are haunting memories of flash floods, people drowning, property damaged........

But a worse memory.......visions of flames peaking over the hills beyond my house......as if on the edge of a volcano......sudden evacuations.............lost lives of people trapped in their garage.

The vision of a firestorm racing north in a deadly cloud.........crowded, unplanned evacuations..............

Then, only a year later, another deadly firestorm to the north ....

Yes, we will take the present rain to help prevent the years of fire......

Spring and Thoughts of Serpent Love

On occasion, I join some other folk on walks around the Pikes Peak area.

This spring a group was watching for spring events at Fountain Creek Nature Center, south of Colorado Springs.

This preserve is the home of deer, bird, and other wildlife.

On our walk back to the center along the canal, someone noticed a snake on the side of the path. Fearing a rattler, someone said that it was a bull snake. Anxiety subsided and curiosity set in.

Then NO! There were two snakes wrapped around each other in the grip of love, literally. The male had his jaws clenched around the female's head in desperate hold. They were slowly moving and twisting with the female in her locked position.

The presence of humans did not seem to deter them at all.

After spending some time watching this rather vicious form of amour, we moved on leaving them and wondering how long this love would last.

The Moon and I

On occasion when we have a full moon, I go to sleep in bright moonlight.

The moon brightens my bedroom window from the east.

Sometimes, the light radiates so bright that it pierces the window shades.

I open the shade to relax in this bright silver light as it washes into my bedroom.

As the night progresses, the moon is high over my roof, but still is penetrating the shades and lighting the ground outside. It moves toward the skylight in my bathroom and glows on me as I get a nightly water glass.

Often, when I wake in the morning, it is still there, lowering itself behind the hill above my house.

People say one gets crazy with a full moon. But I feel these moonlit nights are blessed. The silver beams give comfort and warmth to the night which is often dense and threatening.

The Brave New Mother

It has been a very cold and wet spring.

Each day I look out at the aspens through my tall arched staircase window. The passing seasons often bring joy when the leaves spring forth and the sadness to see them blow away in the fall.

These quaking leaves protect from the western summer sun, and form a lattice pattern in winter.

The monstrous spring storm came about three weeks ago. I have never seen such a strong storm here in the Peak area.

First came the rain, then the hail amidst unbelievable thunder, lightning, and wind. Soon the heavy snow flakes began. The storm lasted for hours.

After the storm cleared the next morning, several inches of frozen ice covered the trees, ground and streets.

A few days later, I was in the front of the house and saw some scraggly branches in one of the aspens. A worker who was there said, "Shall I knock down those twigs?" I said no.

Then, after a couple days, I saw a robin sitting in the tree. Robins don't usually come to my yard. She came again, and I finally realized she had planted her nest in a high crook of the aspen tree.

And so she sits today after a couple of weeks.

She is too high up for me to see more than her head and beak and tail protruding from the nest.

She is there day and night, leaving only for short intervals to presumably feed. On occasion, she gets up and repositions herself.

Another robin was visiting her one day. It is said that the male robin helps in rearing the young, but I have only seen that chap once.

We had another wicked storm last week. I was quite worried. She was there in the morning and ever since.

A neighbor says that the jays get the robin eggs. But I think she is quite smart. The bird feeders for the grosbeaks, jays, flickers, chickadees, and tanagers are in the back of the house. She has her nest in the front. I don't see other birds there.

Will she have a successful nest? I hope so. She certainly is a determined mom.

The First Time...Again!

The Garden of the Gods is two miles from my house, an ancient seabed risen to form a rock garden of magnificence.

On a way to a meeting on a snowy day, I thought, "Why wait to go through the Garden of the Gods later? Do it now!!!!"

How will the snowy road be in the park? The highway would be safer, but not as beautiful!

Driving up the south entrance, there it is, the famous Balanced Rock. But now there are *no* people there. A place that usually has humans crawling all over it was empty and quiet. That grand hunk of rock has just a covering of fresh snow. The red rock appears to have icing with the thin snow layer.

Glad I thought to bring the camera…just a couple of shots here.

The road is snow packed, but plowed, and my Cheroquita has 4 wheel drive.

The morning light is glorious and beautiful on the fresh snow.

Not many people on this road today. But, yes!!!!! Many are also here driving slowly and taking pictures. My goodness, that man is using a tripod in the 10 degree weather. I was not the only one with this thought this morning.

As I drive along, Pikes Peak comes into view with more fresh snow and glows with its beauty, commanding and holding court over the snow covered hills below.

The scrub oak, bare to their branches, twisted and gray, sparkle with their coat of white ice. They huddle together against the great slab of red rock.

The great walls of red of the uplifted sea rock are accented with the fresh white, allowing their massive forms to appear stronger.

The pinon and ponderosa seem strung together with their white blanket. And the great white rock tower is textured with white flakes to create more interest.

Driving north from the park, the whole scene connects….the red formations, green firs, and snowy hills paying homage to the great Peak above.

Although this garden of rock has been loved by me many times, this time was another *first* for me in the Garden of the Gods.

Icicles to Daffodils

Cold and dreary.................snowing for days. One big snowfall, then another,

Then another storm...........No melting.................

And the icicles grow, and grow, and grow......one foot, two feet, three feet and more...............

Then they drip, drip.....drip during the day................then freeze again at night....

Then the dripping becomes loud, and damaging.........running into the ground and down into the cellar onto the floor.

Rescuing the basement from this drip, drip---layers of plastic..........................but still the drips continue.................

BUT: hiding underneath the snow and below the giant icicles appear the green stalks of daffodils..........rather frigid, but green...............

The icicles melt and fall to the ground.................

AND the green stalks grow and grow.....

Finally, a daffodil appears!

Phyllis Joy Sperber

    Phyllis Joy Sperber was born in northeastern Colorado and grew up in the small town of Wray which is nestled in a valley with the Republican River running through it. She attended college at Nebraska Wesleyan University in Lincoln, Nebraska.

    Phyllis enjoyed numerous careers devoting most of her time as an English Teacher, Realtor, Insurance Executive and Life Coach. Education is a primary value evidenced by the number of schools in which she has attended. In addition to Wesleyan, Phyllis has taken classes at Fuller Seminary, Denver University, U.C.L.A., San Diego State, University of Northern Colorado, Arapahoe Community College, Jones Real Estate School and Armbrurst Real Estate Institute.

    She is married to Ray Sperber and has three children: Kim, Brad and Brian. The children, their spouses and her six grandchildren are the sunshine in her life. She currently resides in Colorado Springs and pursues activities based upon building relationships and connecting with people. "Seeing the people" gives her Joy.

Meeting a Friend at Yellowstone National Park

Early in our marriage my husband and I planned a camping trip to Yellowstone National Park. We were both in school, so money was scarce. Early one July morning, we folded our heavy, canvas tent and squashed it into the trunk of our little, red Volkswagen. A cooler with potatoes, eggs and fruit covered half of the back seat; a box containing cooking utensils, including our cast iron skillet, sat on the other half. Clothes lay over the cooler. Most importantly, two fishing poles angled across the entire car. Our pockets held enough money for gas.

I had grown up catching and cleaning trout with my dad. With a fishing pole and a cast iron skillet, Ray and I knew we could compete with any five star restaurant. We were ready for our vacation of the year.

Old Faithful and Yellowstone proved to be as majestic and serene as anticipated. We built fires, watched stars and ate fish. We made sure we caught plenty of fish to take home.

On our last day of vacation we packed the car and doused the fire. The distinctive Volkswagen trunk, located in the front of the car, was loaded with fish. We inserted fish in each nook and cranny of the tent. We were loaded with fish and pictures of fish; we even smelled like fish.

As we drove away from our camp site, I turned to see a bear standing on the site of our former fire pit. "Oh look," I motioned to my husband alerting him to the presence of a cute, little brown bear which had arrived to say goodbye. "Bye for now!" I yelled out the window.

A great idea seized Ray. "I think he would like one of our fish," he exclaimed. Before I could say anything, he leapt from the car and, in a flurry, opened the trunk and tossed a big trout in the bear's direction.

The bear loped toward us in a friendly manner as if it were saying cheerfully, "Wait! I want to go with you!"

At the sight of the oncoming bear Ray began yelling to me to close the car door. My mind raced. I did not want to close the door because I could not fathom leaving my husband alone with a charging bear. I had no clue—until much later when we reconstructed between gasps what had happened—that Ray was mentally telling me to scoot over, open the passenger door for him, close the driver's door then stomp on the accelerator. I froze. The bear's gait intensified, galloping closer. Thankfully, Ray did not panic.

In a flash, he slammed the trunk. Ray moved towards my side of the car then realized I had not moved, and so raced around the entire car and vaulted into the driver's seat. As he slammed his door with a jerk, the bear jumped, landing upon the hood of the red Volkswagen with paws sprawled across the window. His paws touched the windshield wiper blades. We found ourselves staring at our new friend. We looked at the bear and he looked back at us.

"Drive." I yelled. "He wants the fish. Drive!" I screamed again.

Ray started easing slowly forward with the car rocking under the weight of the mammoth, friendly bear.

"Faster," I said. "Drive faster." Our chubby, furry friend soon rolled gently off the car. We did not look back, but as we reached a safe distance, I realized I was sad to leave without a proper goodbye.

A Call from Mom

My mother called last night. When my cell phone's caller ID flashed her name, I abruptly left my church meeting to answer her call.

"Hello. Hello? Who is this?" I asked.

"Hello, Phyllis. Just checking in. Dad and I are on our way home. We spent a few days fishing in Oklahoma and now are on back roads somewhere in Kansas." It had been a long time since I heard her voice but I recognized it in a heartbeat.

Her strong matter-of-fact voice continued, "We are exploring small towns."

"What?" I interrupted. I was stunned. "In Kansas?" I asked.

Mom continued. "Wheat has never looked better. At least three feet tall. Heading out. And the corn. Oh my, it is early. Already peeking out. Maybe three inches tall. Ubiquitous sunflowers. Beauty everywhere. And so green. Must be the rain. All this rain, don't you think, Charles?"

Mom's monologue included Dad which made me realize she was talking to him as much as to me. I pictured Dad driving the '87 blue sedan he bought when he sold cars at Gene Palmrose Ford. Remembering that Dad worked at the car dealer after he retired from teaching called up a picture of Larry, Gene's son who was in school with me; I wondered where he was now. As my mind wandered, Mom continued her travelogue.

"Creeks running high. Milo being harvested early. Look at the windmill and horse tank. Charles, is that electrically powered?" She didn't wait for or expect an answer but described the terrain in terms important only to a country girl. "Hope the farmers don't have hail. Red wheat, I think. Not black."

"Mom. Listen!" I demanded. "Where are you exactly?" I pondered the two of them, these two ninety-seven year old geriatrics driving 40 miles per hour on some desolate Kansas dirt road.

She answered. "Well. I am not sure. We saw a sign for Bethune, didn't we Charles? Or was that today? We stayed at the Broken Bent cabins. Visited nice people in Arcadia. About 250 people live there. Phyllis, can you imagine that we saw a sign in a town that read, Population of One?" Her voice neither wavered nor changed in intensity. I looked at the phone, mesmerized as she rambled on and on. "We had blueberry pancakes this morning in Hope. The waitress was so big and jolly that Dad said she must eat a lot of those pancakes. He even asked her if she devoured pancakes as he paid the bill. So embarrassing." She chuckled softly but there was no pause. "Dad caught the best fish. One rainbow was a beauty. In fact Dad painted a water color of that fish." Then I heard Dad's soft voice offer, "Tell her it was fifteen inches. Tell her that."

I pictured Dad and Mom driving through Kansas. Mom, with faded brown hair, lightly salted, would be wearing a floral cotton dress, nylons and brown shoes with two-inch heels. Her soft round shoulders and rimmed glasses never detracted from her dignified manner. My taciturn dad typically wore a pale blue dress shirt that matched his faded blue eyes, khaki pants and a straw fedora. His silver hair blended with his fair complexion. Strong and fit, Dad always sat erect. He barely moved when driving except to raise a little finger in greeting to each farmer he passed. I envisioned Mom's thoughtful eyes poring over the horizon to smile and greet each person on a tractor in case they needed encouragement.

As Mom's discourse about the countryside hummed along, I moved back to the meeting to see if everyone was still there. Exactly as when I left, Betty talked; others listened. Months of meetings led to this night of decision making. Children sprawled on the floor coloring posters for the big event, scribbling and shading intently under the stern gaze of Vera Boher. Vera crossed her arms and peered over the drawings with never a doubt that she bore her name well. She was bored. All seemed normal; even Henry, with red and green crayons stuck up his nose, focused on the project. Welcome signs covered the floor.

All was serene. Even Mom and Dad meandering through the country fishing for trout seemed peaceful. I pictured the routine.

Dad fished. Mom read. Each night they fried fish he caught, played Scrabble followed by Cribbage. I had read the recorded scores and I knew their competition mounted over the years. As my neurons returned focus to the present moment, Mom's voice recaptured my attention. She explained a biography she was reading about Abigail Adams. She talked about the Wray town news. About Dad's garden. About their neighbor Lillie's arthritis. About Uncle Gus who lived in a one bedroom house behind their Cape Cod. About Grandma Brown's bad knees. About the mosquitos in Oklahoma. I walked outside the building determined to focus upon this conversation from Kansas.

Suddenly I heard silence. Then she asked me a question, "What is it you are trying to decide tonight? Is that meeting important?"

Puzzled. I thought. How does she know I am in a meeting? But I didn't ask. I answered. "This is the final meeting before the annual church banquet Saturday."

"Oh. Oh, yes," she said. "We host bridge that night. I am making a chocolate pie. Dad's favorite, you know. Wanda is bringing orange jello; Thelma is making her sausage rolls." And then, as if she remembered she were talking with me, she asked, "Did you tell me WHY you are in a meeting?"

"We are deciding the color scheme. You know, should we have red or blue napkins or a combination. Things like that." I answer.

Mom muttered, "That is stupid. So what? Who cares?"

Without hesitation, I giggled. "You are right. Who cares?" Maybe Betty. Yes, definitely Betty. I laughed again. "You just used the exact phrase Lowell said when I talked of trivialities or ever complained about anything. He gave me many lectures about the value of meetings. Lowell especially did not tolerate complainers. I started to give an example of an interaction with Lowell, but I caught myself. Would the mention of my late brother's name bring sadness to Mom? She did not reflect on Lowell or my giggling. She just changed the subject.

"Did you see the National Spelling Bee? Hard words. Dad and I thought of you when we watched. We only knew a few. Rapprochement. Pyopoiesis. Pampootie. Ephelides. Ctenoid. Porwigle. Good words. Did you see it?"

"No, I missed it." I said. "Maybe next year." My mind wandered back to my spelling days. Then I heard Mom describe the Jersey cows on the road. I focused on her voice. Totally. I listened. I wanted to record each word. And I realized I did not know my cows very well.

Dad entered the conversation in a determined, loud voice.

"Hey. Look at that sign. Buddy's Burgers. One mile. I am ready for a coke and a burger. Let's stop." Dad displayed a reserved demeanor, but I knew he made the decisions.

Mom acquiesced. "Yes. Let's stop," she said to him. And to me, she softly said, "Well...better go. We will talk soon. I love you. Bye."

Click.

"I love you too," I stammered. But I knew she was gone.

I returned to the meeting as Betty's mouth moved in rhythm with her hands. As I watched her drone on and on, I wondered if I talk with my hands. I knew I did and vowed to break the habit.

As the clock turned slowly, I nodded to Penny, encouraging her, as the chair, to take control. The children continued coloring. The sun dipped behind the Rockies. I was at peace.

Today was a good day.

All was well with the world.

The fact that my parents had been gone over three decades never crossed my mind.

Vacation on Highway 34

Each summer we spent one week in the Colorado Mountains. No discussion occurred because the vacation was routine. Dad and Mom worked as a team. While Mom organized the food and cleaning supplies, not to forget soap and ample rolls of toilet paper, Dad rethreaded fishing poles and secured worms.

The night before we left, Mom instructed each of us five children to fill a flour sack with a few clothes and place it by the front door. Early in the morning we headed west on Highway 34. After a picnic in the Fort Morgan Park and numerous potty breaks, often occurring on the side of the road, we arrived at our destination. The specific rustic cabin and winding river varied, but the actions of my parents never did.

Mom snatched the pail stuffed with rags and Clorox fortified with a broom and mop and entered the germ-filled house. Dad skillfully placed the seven fishing poles against the cabin and guided us children who scampered from the car and down the path to the river. We were never allowed one foot in the dusty hut until Mom thoroughly delivered us from all obscene seen and unseen horrors. After an hour, Dad was requisitioned to carry bedding, pillows and food for a grand entrance into the cabin. The house would be small and cramped, but obsolescence was never a thought. For seven days we owned the land and filled the days by playing, fishing, wading, singing, climbing and laughing. Rocky Mountains. Year after year.

Until.

One day in July Mom and Dad lingered over breakfast. A discussion ensued before Dad turned with a smile and said, "Tomorrow we leave for vacation. We are going to Nebraska to see Great-

Grandma." Mom clapped her hands describing all the fun we would have seeing Great-Aunt Fanny, Great-Uncle Albert and Cousin Sarah Suzanne.

Our little sacks of clothes and the proverbial picnic lunch were the only occupants of the trunk. Fishing poles and cleaning supplies were not mentioned. We headed east on Highway 34.

Catching fire flies and swinging high into the sky from Great-Grandma's tall oak tree are sweet memories from this trip. Occasionally having a turn playing her pump organ made us feel grown-up. That was the only toy in the house, but it offered diversion. Sleeping in a lumpy, feather bed with my siblings was painful. The outside air was sticky and stifling, but the air in the attic on that bed was nonexistent.

What I remember the most from this vacation was the oatmeal. Each morning we sat on a wooden bench around a long, narrow table. In front of each of us sat a bowl. The oatmeal sneered at us; we cowered and ate. Slimy, gooey, gluey cereal. Covered with warm, heavy cream. Each morning we swallowed, nearly gagging to empty the bowl before we could go swing. Only in the past couple of years have I added oatmeal to my diet. Of course, it is now laden with nuts and berries covered with brown sugar. And naturally, no cream, just skim milk.

On the final morning of our vacation, we packed our damp, sweat-lined clothes in our sacks and loaded the car. I ran to the tree for one last finale. I loved that swing. Then out of the house came Grandma.

"You cannot leave without a hearty breakfast. The table is ready. Come."

I winced as Mom agreed; we filed into the kitchen and sat at the table. More oatmeal.

After Grace, Dad said brightly, "Hey, kids. Let's give Mom time to visit with her grandma. Let's take our breakfast outside."

We quickly rose, oatmeal in hand. As soon as we were beyond earshot, Dad said,

"Come by the tree. Quick, give me your bowls." He emptied each bowl in the grass by that big oak tree and after the requisite time, he carried the dishes to the kitchen. I remember waving goodbye to Grandma as we drove away being careful not to look at that tree.

Next year when our annual vacation approached, there was no discussion.

We drove west on Highway 34 to the Rocky Mountains.

Writing is a process,
a journey into memory and the soul.

Isabel Allende

Irmgard von der Gathen

Born and raised in post war Germany Irmgard immigrated with her German husband, Paul, to America by way of a two year residency in Melbourne, Australia, where their first daughter, Janette, was born. Living briefly in San Francisco and Kansas City they decided to settle in Colorado Springs after visiting the mountainous region. Her second daughter was born and grew up in Colorado Springs as well as her three grandchildren.

Irmgard and her husband quickly assimilated and understood the importance of learning English to become successful. Determining that America was their desired new home it was elemental to become US citizens. Irmgard became thoroughly involved in politics and was rewarded with an Outstanding Citizen Award by her chosen party. Besides volunteering for more than 20 years for Silver Key she also lent her help to numerous other organizations.

Yearning for more education which had been elusive in post war Germany, Irmgard entered College in midlife, graduated with honors, and was selected by the board to receive the "Outstanding Student of the Year Award."

With her degree in commercial art she and a partner started an advertising agency and through diligent work and dependability gained respect in the business community. After twelve successful years she sold her business to pursue dabbling in other ventures. Having visited every continent, a special attraction to Italy enticed her to learn its language as well. After accomplishing a fluency in English she decided to write short stories about her childhood and rediscovered her talent for writing. This led her to publishing a book about her mother's and her families' experiences and suffering during World War II.

Having had a rather minimalistic upbringing she values hard work, sincerity in all attempted endeavors and lifelong learning. She now enjoys writing, gardening, traveling and attending lectures of diverse subjects.

Spring

Enough of snow and ice below,
impatiently I count time
for sunshine divine,
to linger, to warm the Earth,
awakening, and giving birth
to new life and end the dearth.

And every day I look around
at what's breaking through the ground.
I like to measure every day
Wishing green wonders would hasten
And burst forth without delay.

Birds are returning in a hurry
fluttering about in a flurry,
gathering things with zest
to feather their nest.
I am ready and eager to toil
and plant anew in my garden's soil.

Daffodils and tulips eagerly show
yellows, reds and pinks in a row.
Followed by lovely purples and blues
of iris and lilac blooming profuse.
Heavenly scents waft in the air,
and leaves are unfolding everywhere.

Summer

And then my favorite season is here,
bringing me the joys of nature
in full glory and every sphere.
Oh, Summer, remain forever here!

From brown earth have grown
miracles of nature, so well known,
and I work in my garden each day
admiring unmatched colors in endless array.

Soft winds carry a pleasant breeze
and I feel heavenly at ease.
Lovely flowers delight my eyes,
and sunshine gives my soul a rise.

Now and then I seek a place of shade,
to sit under a canopy of the richest jade.
And I recline and watch as branches sway
holding too much sunshine at bay.

And then I always wonder about the powers
That gave us boundless designs of trees and flowers.
Oh Summer, delightful season
stay longer and listen to my reason!

Autumn

It is a sad time when fall is here,
because my thoughts of this season
are unlike other people's reason.

Although the colors do delight
I wish with all my might
that lovely summer would remain
with lots of sunshine and some rain.

When there is dew on the ground
I find that leaves and petals
have turned black all round.
Then I know that frost arrived in a rush
and it will turn them all to mush.

Where once beautiful flowers
brightened my garden for many hours,
dazzled my eyes and my senses,
there, tumbleweeds will bounce away
as grass is turning pale to my dismay.

Soon grounds are littered with dead leaves
a cold wind is tucking at my sleeves,
and trees stand bare in lessening light.
For me that is a sad, sad sight.

Winter

Birds departed right on cue,
remaining are just a few.
Fat bears are sleeping in their den,
and horses seek their pen.

Then the dreadful cold sets in
and I wish for the sun to win.
Oh Winter! You are not my friend
and I'm counting the days
when you will end!

But when snow blankets the earth,
hiding the barren fields so brown,
making it all look bright and clean
then how can I still frown?

And when the sun breaks through
giving it all a sparkle and glitter
with air so crisp and and sky so blue
I must reason and not rue.

And then, at least for a while
I'll forget the murky colors below.
I hush in the perfect stillness,
as deer come hither and fro.
But Winter! You cannot beguile!

It Was All Marlon Brando's Fault!

This story is about the invasion of a garment which was, so very ironically, born in Europe. Yes, Europe. I'm talking about the T-shirt mania in America. Oh, give me liberty to share my observations and thoughts on this fashion transgression:

The T-shirt, although it was not yet called by that name, was a standard issue undershirt for European soldiers during World War I. American troops observed and quickly realized how comfortable these lightweight cotton shirts were during hot and humid summer days, or how practical they were for wicking up perspiration under their woolen uniforms. Hence, they wasted no time in christening the undershirt by the now popular name "T-shirt" and by World War II both the Navy and the Army included the white cotton shirt as standard issue.

But back to the part Marlon Brando played in the T-shirt Blitzkrieg. Brando shocked the movie audience by appearing in the white undershirt, sans dress shirt, on the big screen. History was made, when during a steamy scene in the movie *A Streetcar Named Desire* the shirt was torn from his muscular body exposing his chest. Young men all over America promptly discarded their dress shirts and started a new fad by prancing around in their white undershirts, cigarette packs tucked into the rolled up sleeve to boot. In 1955 movie idol James Dean reinforced this cool look in *Rebel without a Cause* and the T-shirt was henceforth ordained as a symbol of rebellious male youth.

In the 1960's, during the time of the tie-dye frenzy, T-shirts proved to be the ideal product on which to experiment. After the immersion into rainbow colors, the Marlon-Brando-look was never the same. By then the shirt was worn as a unisex, all-purpose clothing item, and it blossomed into varieties in the form of tank tops, scoop necks, V-necks. When long sleeves were added and "double knit" was introduced, that variety morphed into what is known by the crass name of sweatshirt.

There was no stopping the proliferation of the clothing market by the T-shirt. It was an inexpensive item, and everyone loved the lazy, comfortable style.

People in the printing business had quickly realized that one could capitalize by printing unlimited images on a T-shirt. Consequently, it didn't take long for rock bands to discover that they could make vast amounts of additional money by selling their motto-emblazoned T-shirts to the willing audience. Professional sport didn't waste time following suit. The Disney Company embellished the shirts with every cartoon character imaginable, and the new billion-dollar enterprise was embraced wholeheartedly as frosting on the cake.

From then on, imagination on what to do with, or to, a T-shirt ran amuck. When other entities, such as record and movie companies, bars, restaurants, animal lovers to computer geeks, and private clubs to universities joined the bandwagon, there was no limit to the oncoming pandemic.

Nor is there any boundary to people's tastes when it comes to wearing the famed shirt. Can one go anywhere to escape the T-shirt-clad torso? One could say that the T-shirts and jeans combination has become America's civilian uniform. Look around you, and you'll find yourself inundated with babies, grandparents, fat and skinny, young and old wearing them. They are worn as day or nightshirts, under or over regular clothing, or two or three at the same time.

It seems to be perfectly acceptable in today's society to wear them in sizes, which have nothing to do with actual body measurements. If it doesn't fit, cut it, rip it, tear out the sleeves, lower the neck line with a quick snip, cut off the bottom to expose the pierced navel, wear them until they are in shreds and the wearer will be instantly in style. Certain types of young men like them triple large, or larger, so they cover the knees, lest their butt crack gets exposed, because they are wearing pants of ridiculously exaggerated sizes, which could slip down and end up around their ankles. Dirty, grimy T-shirts seem to be accepted as just another variety.

"Macho" men, after all those years when they should know better, still think it's "oh, so cool" to roll up a pack of Marlboro in the short sleeve. Some guys even thought they'd make good seat covers by slipping them over the back of a car seat, and almost started a new trend.

Then there are the T-shirts proclaiming messages. Have you read them? They range from stupid to interesting, from tacky to outrageous, from smutty to obscene. I shudder at the sight of some which are imprinted with the most crude gestures and phrases. No matter how offensive, I guess it all falls under the protection of the free speech amendment, and no one was ever arrested for bad taste, as far as I know. But is there anything more egregious than vulgar images worn on ignoramuses' bodies that have become unplugged and gone over the edge?

Clothing designers, who once thumbed their noses at them, have long realized that it is a no-brainer to dupe millions of people to be miniature billboards. Hordes of young people clump around day and night in their logo emblazoned T-shirts, providing the designer and manufacturer with immeasurable amounts of free advertising. Even the formerly hidden labels are now sewn on the outside! Many wearers even think of them as a status symbol. People can be so gullible! Can you count how many of those walking advertisements you see in a day?

What excellent giveaways they make! Since everyone loves a freebie, the giver can get the human sheep to do his advertising easily, and most importantly, cheaply and constantly. Every inch of a T-shirt can now be affixed with logos and jabber-jabber. The front of the shirt no longer suffices. Specialty printers long ago figured out how to imprint the back too. Even the sleeves have lost their virginity!

Young students plague their parents with their choices or their refusal to wear imagined unpopular brands of T-shirts. Principals have an additional and difficult task of getting involved in the fashion world and deciding where to draw the line.

Women, not to be outdone, conjured up innumerable ways to load up, (but not necessarily enhance) a T-shirt. Why not add sequins and glitter; paint whole still-lives on them; sew on buttons, lace, and beads; and heaven forbid, those embroidered flower-like things; and top it off with some fake fur? There is just no end to it. Don't have enough ideas to keep up with the trend? There are galleries of books available on just that subject. Imagine! There is literature on how to decorate T-shirts! And these hideous fandangles don't come cheap. The more thingamajigs and doodads are added, the more dollars are spent. Heck, the shirts could be called diversified portfolios. Tacky, tacky, tacky.

Was it women or men who came up with the "brilliant" idea of the wet t-shirt contests, or is the movie industry to blame again? Silly question. It's got to be men!

There is no end to people who deliberately want to look absurd or be extreme. It crosses all ethnic groups and economic classes. I have a difficult time understanding the person who walks next to someone wearing a T-shirt imprinted with an arrow pointing his or her way saying, "I'm with stupid!" And why does a young woman think she has to draw attention to her abdomen with an arrow on her oversized T-shirt pointing down to the word: Baby? Why does she think the world must know that she is pregnant? Is the onlooker supposed to acknowledge, inquire, or even care?

Oh horror! They have multiplied into epidemic proportions! They are everywhere in the world! No country has been spared the invasion! Even the formally fashion-conscious youngish population of Europe is caught up in this fashion lunacy. I could hardly tell the European males from the American ones, with the exception that those foreigners do stop short of mutilating their shirts or wearing dirty ones. Even the poorest of the poor nations somehow manage to acquire enough T-shirts for the natives to replace traditional garb or cover their formerly unclad bodies. Has there ever been a garment with such short history that has spread and conquered the world, without resistance, in such a quiet coup d'état? Whereto have the nonconformists disappeared?

I am left with the only option of simply accepting this amazing and sometimes freakish turn in fashion or lapse in good taste. I may mock them, or be dismayed by them. I may wish for T-shirt etiquette, requirements for cloaking the indelicate torsos, or a T-shirt police. It's of no use!

The invasion is here to stay.

No Eyes

The old men stand at busy corners, leaning against the wall with their hands held out. Others are sitting on the ground or on wooden crates, hand extended in familiar gesture. I encountered them in busy areas such as the town's market place and along crowded, narrow lanes. They need lots of passing human traffic, because not many people drop a coin into their withered hands.

Now again, I see them in Marrakech in the town square called Djema El Fna, the largest open market center and tourist attraction known throughout Morocco. It's a huge irregular space surrounded by a variety of buildings. The entire space is crowded with a mélange of vendors, beggars, story tellers, an outdoor dentist, fortune tellers, singers, dancers, snake charmers, tourists, endless oddities ...and old men without eyes.

I cannot pass them without putting a coin or two into their bony hands. Such a pitiful sight to my seeing eyes. I wonder, do they really have no eyes? The cavities are there, sunken, eyelids shut. Upon inquiring with our guide, I am told, that this was a disease, brought on by flies laying their eggs into the eyes. Can that be? I don't quite comprehend, but do I really want to know more about it? I don't think so. We must get more change tomorrow. I never seem to have enough coins.

Now they are everywhere, standing there in the middle of the alleys, in their long dirty caftans, holding a tall walking stick and a small plastic bowl. Some are banging the bowl against their sticks, to attract more attention. Most are lamenting something undecipherable in unrelenting monotone. Without exception, they nod their heads when receiving a token. They palpate the coin and mutter an indistinct response.

And then the hand with the coin is swift. It knows exactly the place where it's supposed to go. With great celerity it disappears quickly under the caftan and just as quickly is ready to take its position again, out there in front of the body of the men without eyes.

Back to the Middle Ages

Up a dimly lit, narrow, and crooked stairway we tread, not knowing what lies ahead. Then we reach the roof terrace and exit into bright daylight. It's like stepping out of a time machine, having been transported back to the Middle Ages! There, before our eyes, in the immense courtyard below are rows of containers, side by side, filling the whole area. The pond-like receptacles built out of mud and clay bricks, run several feet in diameter and depth. They are filled with an array of indistinguishable liquids, dirty water and various shades of dyes.

Men are perched on the rims, climbing about like storks, or standing in the round containers stomping on, or wringing out pieces of leather. Others are spreading straw wherever there is a rooftop or flat surface, to lay out the already dyed skins to dry.

Now I see the awful looking, bad smelling mules arriving loaded with raw animal skins. Earlier, down below in the narrow alley, they squeezed by us, making us jump eagerly out of the way, pressing ourselves against the walls, to avoid being touched by this stinking, dripping load.

Even though I am feeling nauseous my curiosity holds me spellbound as our guide explains the operation that's going on before our eyes.

The scantily clad men must first remove the hair before the animal skins are thrown into a calcium solution, there to remain for three to four weeks. After that the hides are rinsed with water and the tanners must stomp on them day after day, bare-footed, until the hides are soft.

Then the evolving leathers are soaked in a solution made from pigeon dung and rinsed again. Next, they are dyed with natural or chemical colorants and finally treated with tannin. Our tour guide also explains that the natural dyes are mixed with cow urine due to the dearth of water. It makes me contemplate – how much the human skin can endure!

Now, imagine the combined odor of raw animal skins, tannic acids, cow urine, the brew of pigeon dung, and top it off with the sweat of the unwashed male bodies and what do you get? A bestial stink that cannot be described in any words!

After enduring this assault on all my senses, and witnessing this torturous laboring, in a setting frozen in time, I will never look at leather goods made in Morocco the same as before.

Marge Zimmerman

Marge Zimmerman was born in Galveston, Texas, but for the last 10 years has lived in Colorado Springs, Colorado. Before that she lived in Maryland for 33 years.

She has a Bachelor of Arts from the University of Maryland at College Park with a concentration in Urban Studies. She received a Master of Social Work from the University of Maryland, Baltimore with a concentration in Social Work and Community Planning.

She worked at a mental health center for ten years and had a private psychotherapy practice for 15 years. She has now retired to travel, garden, read, hike, quilt and enjoy the cultural arts.

She has three grown children and seven grandchildren.

Fear

He came like a ghost
    Almost invisible
He crept closer
    Inching into my space
Magnetic things happening
    No control
I'm lost.

With one word came the fear
    Gripping my gut deep
No logic to this happening
    Only the knowing that it came from a past experience
Long ago.

Shadows cast their lines
    Cutting off the sun's rays.
Which leaves me wondering when will the light shine again.

Death

Death – such a final act. But is it?? Or is it merely a transition from one spiritual place to another?

For many years death was a taboo subject. But over time, the topic has opened up new realms of investigations, both medically and spiritually.

Recently I have been brought face-to-face with unexpected deaths. Many friends are making their passing.

Death mostly comes as a shock, sometimes it comes as an awaited announcement. The questions I ask myself are: is it better to know ahead of time that death is coming (as happened with Joan S.) or is it better to have a swift exit (as happened with Ann N.)?

Ann had such a peaceful passing formula: she just went to sleep, breathing aided by a C-PAP machine and never woke up.

But this also leaves the living wishing they'd had a few last words or a tearful goodbye.

Most recently a friend's 44 year old son struggled to his end in a hospital room attached to many machines until his organs stopped functioning. It seemed there was a resistance and a difficulty letting go.

Recently I had the experience of a close call with death by a sudden health crisis. Experiences seem to arise to give us the opportunity to learn lessons for our spiritual growth and awareness. What were my lessons learned? First, to explore how I am living each day. Is it with gratitude? Second, am I living my life fully with an open heart? Third, am I letting go of fear for something I have no control over (when death is coming and how that will happen). Now I will cultivate a greater openness to the unknown and participate each day of my life more fully and celebrate each moment as a gift. So frequently the unexpected or the unwanted brings each of us to that door of passing. I would like to approach this point of the inevitable with peace and acceptance.

At services for those friends and acquaintances who have passed, I realize that I have not put in writing what my desires are when I die. But my imagination goes to a picture of a celebration after my death of a joyful gathering of family and friends with good food and plentiful drink to toast in my memory.

There is no other preparation for death except opening to the present and living life as an adventure.

Galveston

First it was just an island, a stretch of sand surrounded by the Gulf of Mexico. It is said that the first inhabitants were the Karankawa Indian tribe.

Then, Spanish explorers noted the presence of the island around 1519/1520.

Cabeza de Vaca was stranded there with about 80 Spaniards after being swept ashore by a storm which wrecked their boat around 1528. At this time the island was called Malhado but because of many snakes reported on the island it was often referred to as Isla de Culebras (Island of Snakes).

In about 1817, Jean Lafitte, the pirate (or privateer as he is sometimes referred to) probably was the first to refer to the island as Galvezton (later spelled Galveston). Myth was that Lafitte buried treasure there but none has ever been found.

My first family member to land on the island was my great-grandfather, Capt. James McDonald who came from Scotland in the mid-1800's. He was captain of his own sailing vessel and later became harbor master. Newspaper clippings from The Galveston News gave interesting facts about his civic and political involvements.

Other relatives from at least four different countries followed as Galveston was a port destination for many immigrants coming to start a new life.

The entry to the island was once by boat only, but now a causeway spans the water, high enough for boats to pass under.

You can smell the fragrant oleander blossoms as you enter the city. They are planted on a wide esplanade interspersed by tall palm trees which leads the visitor eventually to the Gulf beaches. There is a salty smell in the air which increases the closer you get to the water. There is abundant seafood which carries a Gulf-flavor. You can see the shrimp boats from the boulevard which borders the south side of the island beaches. One can go down to the wharf on the other side of the island to see the boats unloading their catches for restaurants and buyers to carry home.

Galveston is also well known for the historic hurricane of 1900 which hit the city with little notice. It took the lives of between 6000-9000 residents.

Clara Barton traveled to Galveston to nurse the injured in one of the few buildings left standing, the Ursuline Academy (a large Catholic school).

I am aware of one family member who drowned during this hurricane. She was my grandmother's sister, Anna, who died with her unborn child. The story is that she slipped from a roof where she and her husband had climbed to escape the rising and raging water, leaving her distraught husband clinging for his life. He survived.

After the water subsided and the clean-up began, the U.S. Corp of Engineers. proposed raising the entire city, therefore preventing future flooding. Every structure left standing was raised and landfill brought in.

The second major effort was the building of a seawall along the shore facing the Gulf. The original seawall is still standing, having stood the test of time and many hurricanes that followed.

As a child I loved to walk the streets to admire the beautiful Victorian homes - some large, some small. I also loved to walk the beach, remembering the many footsteps which had been there before mine:

Native Americans, Spanish, French, English, German and Norwegian; young, old, wealthy and poor immigrants, leaving their mark on this small island in the Gulf of Mexico.

Four generations of my family have been born on the island, although none of my family lives there now. The family home still stands in great disrepair.

But there is no doubt that when I return the spirits of long departed relatives linger and seem to whisper in my ear, "Welcome back."

The Storm

The storm clouds were building, large, black and gray with hints of purple and a green cast over everything. Wind movement was constantly changing the shape of the landscape. The horizon almost entirely disappeared in the darkness which was rapidly approaching – an ominous, eerie backdrop of nature changing and churning her powerful forces.

Where to go? What to do? No time to plan; only act. Fear is a strong motivator when one is being threatened. Life's experiences flash like a fast-forward movie along with those things not done, things on my bucket list.

Why was I so cautious earlier in life? Have I missed opportunities to do the wild and crazy things I often dreamed about? Have I lost the option to follow the impulsive acts which would have taken me to new places and exciting adventures?

Taking shelter quickly, I waited for the burst of tragedy, fear heightening. Then a heavy silence – a quietness, too quiet to believe. Has it passed?

What was all the worry about? Now I can go back to my rituals of sameness, content to follow my normal routine. Life is good just the way it is. I can breathe easy now.

The Threat

A chill rolled over me as I sat on the sandy bank of shoreline. The fog moved in from the dark water – the darkest I have ever experienced. The fog kept advancing, bringing in a thickness like molasses.

The hairs on my arms stood on end; my scalp twitched with a fear never experienced before. My whole body vibrated with an electricity which said: "*Run*, you fool!"

But I couldn't move. I was frozen there on this sandy spot totally enveloped by a heaviness, like a prisoner.

My heart began beating louder and louder until my throat felt almost blocked by its echo.

Is this possible? Could this be happening to me?

The wind whistled, an ominous sound, blowing from all directions.

Footsteps are muted by the soft sand and I am too frightened to look behind me.

I keep replaying the threat in my mind, "Beware the darkness and a stranger lurking." What does that mean?

I feel a scream bubbling up from my throat.

Suddenly a hand grabs my trembling arm. The words come: *Wake up Marge! It's only a dream.*

The Waldo Canyon Fire

The exit was swift and hectic
No time to waste
What is of importance here?

The rational mind is not working
Too frazzled to comprehend the danger.

Flames grabbing each blade
Too fast for the eye to follow
Smoke travels faster than time itself

Leaving a scorched earth
Sooty and barren
And many lessons for the unprepared.

Judith McKay

Life's journey began in Ohio
In a beautiful countryside area near the city.
The eldest of four siblings, life was never dull,
Filled with roller coaster rides and
Smooth sailing seas.

Writing began with a diary given by my grandmother.
Then journals came and the Artist Way and Morning Pages,
And writing began expressing itself,
Along with music and art.
Offered a job in England as an Accountant and Financial Manager
The world was at my fingertips.
Little did I know my future husband was to be there –

Discovering various forms of writing,
Dialogue became fun and a play was born,
And a thespian sprouted her wings.
Then Haiku showed up,
Who would have guessed?

Being a curious person
with a penchant for learning
in the classroom and the world –
new landscapes, cultures and traditions
meeting new people –
has been a grand and glorious
experience and education.
My journey continues to unfold and open to
new challenges and new opportunities –
And what a journey!

Musings from the Park Bench

– can conjure up new views if one is open to seeing
– can conjure up memories if one is open to listening
– can conjure up new feelings of being alive and grateful
– can conjure up a stillness that can speak to your heart and soul

1. **The Park Bench overlooking the Pacific Ocean** beckoned to me shortly after I arrived. An invitation to the beautiful southern California coast was received with an exhilaration I hadn't felt in a long time. I think it was because I needed to have a change of scenery – albeit a vacation of just relaxing and not having to stare at a house full of boxes just received from the moving company. Making a major move can be taxing, to say the least, although my husband and I were excited about starting a new chapter in our lives. What we were leaving was one of very satisfying work, good friendships and involvement in community. It had been a marvelous experience living in this community by the water with a view of the mountains. And there was a wholesale seafood shop just an esplanade walk away. It couldn't get much better. I knew I had been blessed, and always said a big thank you every time I walked back home with my little brown bag of something delicious from the ocean.

Being a curious person, I looked into some research engines about the area we were going to be staying for a week. My husband's company was sending him to a week-long workshop at a resort overlooking the Pacific Ocean and he wanted me to go along. It was my choice of course to stay home or go, but how could a girl turn down such an invitation – no work and all play, and lots of relaxation. Enjoying the fare of a first-class chef at this resort was another one of my senses to be gratefully and deliciously satisfied. Extraordinary scenery as I was discovering in my search was what really set my heart on fire to accept this invitation. A new adventure began.

The cool sea breeze brushing against my skin and the sun shining through the beautiful wispy clouds, I skipped across the beach, the sand between my toes and feeling a strong connection to the earth, barefoot and happy. The sound of the surf along with the call of sea gulls hovering above continued to make this moment very spiritual and peaceful. I was happy. Checking my surroundings I seemed to be the only person around. In other words, I was the only one to be enjoying this extraordinary scenery.

A beautiful wooden bench appeared around the bend as I continued walking on this pristine white sand. I decided to carve something beautiful in the sand, not for posterity as it would quickly disappear when the tide came in, but as a spiritual connectedness. Even though I enjoyed the walk the sight of the bench looked inviting for a moment of contemplation while taking in this powerful yet serene landscape. The landscape continued to gently rise and the sandy beach began to turn into a pebbly surface and then grasses and wildflowers beckoned in the distance.

Finding myself becoming totally at one with my surroundings while sitting on this well-worn bench, an unusual stillness and light began surrounding me. I looked up and someone I didn't recognize sat down beside me. I hadn't even heard this person approach the bench. An awkward moment of silence persists in what seems like hours as I waited for a question, a comment. He just sat there very calmly dressed in a white flowing robe and sandals with sun-darkened skin. A sense of safety and comfort quieted my questioning mind.

Finally, I asked who he is and what he was doing here. He is my teacher. After discovering that, I became fidgety. What does he really want? After a few more uneasy moments, I quieted my mind and attempted to remain in that quiet place.

Then out of this peaceful moment that I was finally able to get myself into, he looked at me and began cracking jokes that were filled with words of wisdom. He said that it is surprising what one can learn when relaxed and laughing – when one lets themselves open to learning. He had the most beautiful gentle smile with a hint of mischievousness and a laughter that could be heard all the way to Japan, so I thought. At first I was startled at this loud outburst, but it was a genuine kind of laughter that made me feel all was well, and that I was not being put to a test.

He began telling me a story that contained snippets of my life. My mother and dad made an appearance and then my grandparents, and then my brothers and sister. How does he know what I think is my story? He continued on through my school years, playing the clarinet in the high school band – loving it and hating it at the same time. My parents thought I should do this. I was not destined to be a great clarinetist. The story continued as I travelled to New York City and Washington, DC twice with my high school class and once with an invitation to travel with another senior class. Then on to my first job, and on and on he goes, telling me more than I hoped to hear, spot on. Second job, and education classes continued because I love to learn, being that curious gal. I always liked to change jobs once I learned what "made them tick". After all, I was young, single and invincible. All was well – almost.

Then he got down to the nitty gritty, saying that I hadn't totally forgiven my dad, even though I said I had. During my early career years of still getting my "feet wet," I told my parents that I had convinced the owners of a very prestigious family-owned travel agency to teach me to be a travel agent so that I could travel around the world scoping out places to send their clients. I knew that's what I wanted to do. I was so happy when I was telling this story to my parents. My dad looked right at me and said, "You don't want to do that, get a real job, save your money and then travel." And so I did. Being the eldest child, I knew my parents knew best. I remember that as if it happened yesterday. I have been fortunate to have many opportunities to travel and live in other countries since then. Of course I will never know what that would been like to have had a full-time career being happily ensconced in a real live dream come true.

In that moment with that smile on his face staring at me with no judgment, I got the message. I felt like I wanted to give him a big hug and also have a cry as I felt a number of emotions at that moment – relief, sadness of not understanding until now and having wasted all this time fretting. I did neither. I felt lighter than I ever had. I just sat there, forgave myself and my dad, and knew that all was well.

And then, without more than a thank you, a blessing and a beautiful smile, he was gone.

There was nothing in sight – no boat, no building. I knew I had an active imagination and had always been very curious about life. Was this a mirror I was looking into or was the energy of the sea getting to me? I don't think so. I think I had been given one of those special moments – a gift of a lifetime.

Unexpected things can happen in two's or more. Shortly after I returned home, a person that I did not know came up to me. She acted like she knew me and when the occasion presented itself, I told her the same story about the travel agent, and she said, "You know your dad was looking out for your best interests. He only wanted the best for you and that's what he knew. Be thankful that he cared that much." The same thing I had heard earlier. I learned to trust.

As I continue to learn, I know that life is a journey to enjoy, give thanks, be kind and love every moment that I am given. I also know that the people that cross my path, even for a moment, are there to guide and teach, no matter how that presents itself.

2. **The Park Bench by the Lake.** The retired gentleman always took his morning constitutional walk through the park near his home. He felt good being there – he was stimulated just by the energy of the park. His favorite place to contemplate the day and his life was at the park bench overlooking a pristine lake with a view of a mountain range in the background. The lake was brilliantly blue this morning, almost radiating the same color of the sky. The sun was climbing higher, even though it was only 8:30 this particular morning. Usually he liked to be on his walk by 7:00, but this morning – well, he had a lot on his mind and just seemed to be going in slow motion. It was to be a fun day – doing something unexpected. An old acquaintance had called him out of the clear blue, inviting him to meet him for a cup of coffee at 10:00 a.m. to catch up on old times.

He hadn't seen Joe in over five years when they had crossed paths with a mutual business partner. Joe had always been somewhat of a gambler and fussbudget but always seemed to be very pleasant with a good head on his shoulder. There was definitely something to like about him, though they had never formed a close bond.

So this morning he was a bit apprehensive, but still he thought, "why not see what happens. Maybe I need to start reaching out more since I have more free time on my hands." And then he realized why he was apprehensive. There had been a big scandal five years ago when the company Joe worked for discovered they were being embezzled. The case was never solved. Shortly after that, he remembered reading in the paper that Joe had retired. Joe's name made the paper because he had been the CFO of the company for well on to 25 years. "So now here he is calling me. What on earth for? I guess I will find out."

3. **Sing Your Song at your Favorite Park Bench.** "How does that sound, Maddy?" her friend asked. Maddy had always been rather

shy and the thought of going to her favorite park bench by the gurgling stream and pristine forest gave her heart joy to just sing to the heavens, as if no one was listening. And yet deep in her heart she hoped that today with this invitation that just the right person would be listening, and her life could be transformed from her dreams into reality. Her dream was to be a famous singer, for she knew she had the voice. But her life had been fraught with lots of turmoil, and the opportunities had been very few. So with this kind, unexpected invitation from her dear friend, Maddy thought to herself, "why not go one more time to my favorite park bench where I always feel at peace and just sing and give thanks." And so she said yes, and never looked back.

4. **Reflections at the Garden Bench.** As I had some time before my hair appointment, I decided to take a walk in the early morning before it got too hot, even though 8:30 was not that early. As I had a few moments of cool fresh air before the sun became too intense, I stepped up my pace. A Gothic-designed church came into view with a beautiful green lawn and a garden with a statue of a saint holding a bird, water fountain and brightly colored flowers dotting the surrounding space. The circular brick path going around this garden had park benches offering views from all directions. Red roses cascaded along a metal fence behind this garden. The scene was so inviting I couldn't help but stop and sit a spell.

Sitting on the bench, I began reflecting on the day ahead and the book project I had so enthusiastically agreed to participate in. I felt like I had all the time in the world to write my "masterpiece" until I realized only two weeks remained before the deadline. I had not written one word of the allowable 3,000 words. Time to get serious.

So as I sat on the park bench with the sun shining gently over me and the big church standing off in one corner in this picturesque scene, I found myself melting into this space as the busyness and noise outside this garden ceased to exist. I felt a peace come over me that almost lulled me to sleep. I lost all thought of time and was being gently transformed into this quiet stillness. Though I didn't have any paper or even a pen to write with, I felt the words coming and hoped I could remember them later. And then out of the clear blue, a loud noise broke the stillness and I was brought back to this noisy reality. Looking at my watch, I jumped up and dashed off to my hair appointment, arriving not a minute too early.

The words and thoughts remained until I sat in front of my laptop. My time was rapidly running out. Deadlines. They keep me honest and on time.

5. **Dream Your Dreams at the Bench of Wisdom.** I knew I was to go to this old cement park bench today, though I didn't know why. It is a place I often sought out when I wanted to spend time to dream and relax. The bench has poets' words of wisdom carved into various places and made me feel that maybe some of this wisdom would rub off. It is in a quiet place by a church with a beautiful old tree behind it, the branches cascading out in all directions, providing a comfortable shade and protection from the hot summer sun. As I sat there, thoughts of a dear friend who had recently made her transition came to mind. She was very wise for her age even though she wasn't old; in fact we were the same age minus a few months. Some of her qualities that attracted me were her quiet wisdom, her enormous sweet laughter, the twinkle in her eyes, and her playfulness. We had met in a church group and then became friends in a women's group, and through that our friendship continued to grow, and we began to discover many things we had in common.

One of the things we shared for at least three years was singing in a community chorus. We would sing at retirement homes many times during the year and that always brought humbleness and a heartfelt gratitude. The city's annual Christmas Tree Festival at the Convention Center was a moment to get caught up in the season with the festivities of song and beauty. That was quite the gala as people came from far and wide to see the incredibly beautiful decorated Christmas trees and be entertained by various musical groups.

She had also invited me to spend a week together at a retreat in Malibu, CA. Too bad. Someone had to go to the Pacific coast again. It was even more than I could have dreamed, not just the scenery but the week-long spiritual exploration. Meeting new people and making friends was also a pleasure, plus eating fresh seafood. How I adored all of those things. As I think about these moments we shared, I find myself being taken to the park bench sitting on a point overlooking the Pacific Ocean. I can still see the images of the sunsets, the variety of trees, myriad of flowers and plants, the sound of the surf, and the aroma of eucalyptus wafting through the air. I could have sat there for hours. Oh, the memories as they continue permeating my heart. I miss her deeply. For she was not only an inspiration, she was a good listener, kind and considerate, and she knew how to live richly and simply. She had asked me to write a play of her story, of which she had shared only snippets. Maybe I knew more about her than I realized, and even more about me.

When you dream on a park bench, you never know where you might be lead. And so the adventure continues.

The last thought for the day –

Park benches can show up in unlikely places
Old or new they beckon to me
Like a friend waiting to greet me
Folding me in their arms and
Filling me with a happiness
Like I have never known.

Janet Condit

Janet was raised on a strawberry farm in Oregon, where she learned how to work hard, sew her own clothes, and make jam. She studied mathematics and computer science, but postponed her career when she married Jim Condit, an Air Force pilot. As a military family, Janet and Jim and their two children lived in England, Italy, and several states. They eventually settled in Colorado Springs, having decided it was the perfect place to be. They vowed never to move again, but quickly abandoned that pledge when Janet was offered a job in Europe. After six years in Holland, Janet and Jim returned to Colorado Springs to stay – except when they are traveling. Janet's favorite pastimes are hiking, skiing, reading, playing the flute, and watching her two grandsons grow up.

The Summer Quilt

When life throws you scraps, make a quilt.

"Just step into this broom closet and take off all your clothes," said the stone-faced nurse. Her tone of voice convinced me that I should do as I was told. Medical and cleaning supplies filled the closet shelves and in one corner a couple of mops languished in a metal bucket. There was nowhere to hang my clothes as I disrobed, so I folded them carefully and laid them on a shelf. It was chilly in the cramped, dimly-lit space. I started to shiver, whether from the temperature or fear or anger, I couldn't tell.

This was not what I imagined when I eagerly accepted a job in Holland. I envisioned a glamorous life, shopping for local cheeses in charming Dutch villages, bicycling through fields of tulips, and thriving in a career-enhancing position working with European scientists and engineers. Never mind the moments when I would be lost or confused, or misunderstand the customs and language. It was going to be exciting and fun! But now, as I stood there in the closet of a foreign hospital, cold, naked and afraid, I had only one thought: *I want my mommy!*

Due to an administrative glitch, no changing rooms were available at the Dutch hospital where I was to undergo a diagnostic cardiac procedure. With no apology offered, Nurse Stone Face handed me a gown and then escorted me down the hall to the operating theater. After the procedure, a kindly doctor gave it to me straight: "You have a heart condition. It's serious."

How could this be? I was barely 50! I'd hardly been sick a day in my life! It hadn't even occurred to me that I might need major medical care in Holland. I was soon confronted by frustrating delays and a confusing bureaucracy of Dutch health care regulations in a language that I had not quite mastered. In the end, I decided to return to the United States for treatment – I did, in fact, go running home to Mommy!

How lucky I was to have my mother (and father) to run home to! They still lived in the farmhouse in Oregon where I grew up. They were not only prepared to take me in, but also to arrange appointments with their own cardiologists for their ill and somewhat frightened daughter.

It was a pleasant summer day when I arrived. The first thing Mom did was set up an old lounge chair under a tree in the back yard and insist that I recline there to be waited upon. To make the chair more comfortable, she produced an old quilt from the back of a closet and spread it on the chair. As I leaned back onto the softness of the quilt, I felt my apprehension recede. I understood immediately why a thick quilt like this was called a "comforter."

I spent almost three months on the farm that summer, recuperating after a successful treatment of my condition. At first I worried about living with Mom and Dad for such an extended period. After I left home at the age of 18 to attend college, visits with my parents never lasted longer than a week. What if Mom and Dad got sick and tired of me? What if I got sick and tired of *them*? But I needn't have been concerned. We found things to do together, time to talk. I asked questions about my ancestry and we pored over old photo albums. I learned much about my family's history as the summer progressed.

As the weeks passed, I got to know the quilt well as it followed me from the lounge chair under the tree, to the living room, and back outside again. On warm days I lay on top of the quilt, its padding providing a soft cushion. On chilly evenings, I drew it around me for warmth and comfort. The hand-made quilt had belonged to my great-grandmother Bartlett and was passed down to my paternal grandmother, and then to my parents. Its flower-shaped patchwork pattern was composed of scraps of multi-colored cotton. Dating from a time when rural women made their own clothes, I knew the fabrics in the quilt must have come from the clothing my father's ancestors wore.

The well-worn quilt, which was at first my sanctuary, became a project. Some of the patchwork pieces were loose; others were in shreds. In my idle time, I picked up a needle and thread and re-stitched a few of the pieces. But some were beyond repair, so I went in search of fabric to replace some of the worn and missing segments.

Mom came from a long line of seamstresses who never threw away any useful piece of fabric. She eagerly offered up her stash of scraps. As Mom extracted bits of cloth from her stockpile, she described the origin of each one, often with a story attached. There was fabric from her mother's old apron, a piece of cloth from matching dresses Mom and her sister had as young girls, an old skirt, a former kitchen curtain, my younger sister's favorite dress when she was in grade school. I recognized the orange stripes of a dress that I wore on my very first date.

I used Mom's selections to cut new flower-shaped pieces for the quilt. I began stitching them into place, blending these fragments of my mother's history into the framework of the quilt from my father's family.

The task was not quite finished when my doctors declared me healthy and I returned to Holland. I had no further health problems for the rest of my sojourn there, and the experiences of my dream job in Europe enriched my life for several more years.

Many years later, after Mom and Dad had both passed away, I returned to the old farmhouse. I searched for the quilt that had seen me through that long-ago summer. I found it carefully packed away in the attic, still in the same tattered condition as when I had last seen it. Wrapped inside were the replacement pieces I had cut. I didn't want to leave my beloved old quilt to wither in the attic, so I brought it home with me. As I continue to stitch the latest generation of fabric into the quilt, I hope it will be ready to bring solace to a future member of my family whenever the need arises.

Start writing, no matter what.
The water does not flow until the faucet is turned on.

Louis L'Amour

Joyce Aubrey

Joyce's childhood on a small Kansas farm sparked a lifelong appreciation of the simplicity and wonder of nature. From the one-room school where her education began to a Master's Degree and throughout careers of teaching, counseling, and owner/manager of a fabric shop she embedded creative expression in her work.

At fifty-three years old, mother of two grown sons and married for 30+ years, flashbacks to childhood incest invaded her awareness, compromising her ambition, spirituality, even her sanity. Flashbacks revealed abuse that continued for more than a decade and included many perpetrators.

Three years after the first flashback, Joyce was a Colorado Springs resident: divorced, unemployed, her mother deceased, and her brothers attempting to discredit/disown her. Joyce sought healing through traditional and alternative modalities including massage, psychotherapy, Rolfing, myofascial release, chiropractic, naturopathic medicine, rebirthing, acupuncture, and prescription meds, as well as process painting.

As an advocate, Joyce shows how art helped transform incest from a painful past to an empowered present and hopeful future. The goal in process painting is the experience, not the finished product. Like many trauma survivors, Joyce witnessed images emerging from random brush strokes, that revealed scenes trapped in cellular memory and not in conscious awareness.

Today, Joyce enjoys a home surrounded by native flora and tranquil waterfalls. She leads a non-profit "Finding Our Voices" with the mission to empower adult survivors of sexual violence and to advocate for prevention. In addition to speaking and writing of her recovery, Joyce sings, plays piano, and leads process painting.

Story Telling

I have a story to tell; don't know how to do it well
    I'd like to lift my voice and shout,
      but don't know if it's safe to let it out
The sordid things I've done and the dark places I've been
    Maybe you think acknowledging incest is a sin
But I've faced my demons and came out stronger
    My body doesn't ache and weep any longer
My perps can hate me and call me crazy
    But I will NOT be silent, isolated or lazy
I'll speak my truth right out loud
    Heal my wounds and make Little Joyce proud
For I know there's life to be celebrated, joy to be shared
    My abusers will gasp when they learn that I dared
To be all I could be, to stand up tall
    To walk in the light and enjoy it all
My kinfolk are mired in hate, anger and greed
    Why would I follow their lead?
I'll sing in the sunshine and dance in the rain
    Be grateful for love and friendships that keep me sane.
I'll not be silenced by pain and fear
    Doesn't matter birth family if you are far away or near
Little Joyce and I have healed so much
    We've heard the angels whisper and felt their touch
Now we are one and we've begun a shared mission
    This work is our passion, though not for fame or glory
But for the thrill we feel when we empower other survivors
    To break their silence and tell their story

Little Girls Are Like Kittens

Talking about incest memories was difficult for me, even after years of therapy and healing. As a woman of more than sixty years, whose life was shattered a decade earlier by flashbacks, I wanted to reach out to other survivors but didn't know where to start. Initially, much of my confusion was the disparity between recent lurid flashbacks and the authorized version of my childhood that claimed I was a pampered little girl. My parents often told folks "Joycie likes to have her cake and eat it too." Believing that other survivors of trauma who repressed their abuse must grapple with similar inconsistencies, I decided to write my first short story about the occluded part of my youth in the voice of my inner child as she revealed her life experience to me.

The hayloft in the old barn was filled with sights and sounds and smells. It cradled birds and mice, kids and kittens and more. Now it cradled me, lying on my back in wheat straw.

My Daddy's barn reached higher than any other in the neighborhood, as high as the windmill tower. Through the open loft door, a rainbow arched across the Kansas sky, following the afternoon shower like my shadow followed me.

Shadows were my favorite playmates, they reminded me of two things: the one storybook I owned and my Daddy. Robert Louis Stevenson gave me a friend when he wrote: "I have a little shadow that goes in and out with me." I'd read *Child's Garden of Verses* so many times its cover was missing.

My Daddy taught me to sing "Me and My Shadow" before I was old enough to go to the one-room school a half-mile down the dirt road from our farm. "Not a soul to tell my troubles to..." felt real to me on the farm as the little sister of two brothers, one eight years and one 18 months older.

Sparrows in the barn loft, excited by the afternoon rain, squeaked and darted about. A breeze coming through the open loft carried the smell of baled alfalfa from the far side of the haymow to where I rested. The sickening, too sweet odor filled my nose and sunk all the way down to my tummy, making me want to throw up. The smell of new bales in the haymow was heavy, not like blooming alfalfa in the field behind our house that smelled almost like lilacs.

Suddenly the wind howled across the corral and seeped through the old siding, sending a chill through me that jerked my foggy brain awake. The creaking timbers seemed to speak, "Get up little girl, get up Joycie and run."

I pulled my rumpled dress down from my face and rolled away from a gooey puddle on the floor. Looking around, I spotted my undies nearby and wiggled them up over my sticky legs. Scattered wheat straw crackled beneath me and the prickly ends scratched my skin. Funny how a big pile of straw felt squashy when I jumped on it but up close it could jab.

Itchy blotches swelled on my arms from the straw prickles. That nasty red weepy rash had returned. It seemed to hide beneath my skin ready to erupt like a haunting melody that bubbled up and whispered of things not right—of things too scary to talk about yet seeping out of my skin.

I shuddered when I remembered all the cures for rash that weren't really cures. First was Mother's remedy: sour cream poultices applied over the rash with tightly tied rags. Mom said, "Cows cream takes care of sunburns and bee stings, why not this?" The stink of souring cream that got worse with each passing hour made me want to run away from myself.

Then there was Daddy's cure, the purple medicine that healed cows udders and horses sores. It stained my clothes and turned my skin brown as Daddy's fingers that rolled his cigarettes; but it didn't stop my itch.

After I missed a lot of school during first grade my teacher told my folks they should take me to see a doctor. We drove all the way to Junction City to see a specialist whose cures were different than my folks' remedies. The blotches didn't go away when the first doctor used ultraviolet light. He sent us to another doctor who zapped the oozing red patches with ultra-red rays. That was scary. In a room all by myself I had to sit under a heavy lead apron and hold my hands so the red patches were under little holes in the heavy lead thing. My left pinky finger shriveled after that and looked funny. I didn't want to go back to that doctor. He might shrink so much of me that I'd disappear.

Red blotches weren't my only problem; right now I wanted to get down from the haymow and out of the barn. But no one was there to help me down the ladder to the milk barn below. Only moments earlier I sat among the sparrows on the rafters near the roof and watched my winged buddies swoop down to the floor for grain. I almost felt like I was flying with them.

I was usually scared to be up high, like when my brother talked me into climbing the windmill tower. Halfway up I looked down at the ground and got scared. Screaming got my Daddy's attention and he ran from the granary to rescue me. My Dad was big and strong. He would never let anything hurt me.

Sitting on the rafters in the hayloft wasn't scary, like climbing the windmill tower. I never thought about falling when I was high in the barn beside the birds. It's like I was blanketed in something soft and warm and held secure by someone I couldn't see.

While I was perched on the rafters I heard voices below, men's voices. But they were not talking normal talk. They made sounds more like hogs made when they wallowed in the mud—a grunting kind of noise. The men took turns pushing hard, sort of on their knees. After their work they breathed hard and stretched out on the straw to rest. I guess they worked really hard.

A voice in my head said, "Enough daydreaming." That voice sounded like Mother. She always told me that. I tried to remember why I was in the haymow. Looking for someone to help me, I peered all around—up at the rafters, across the hay bales to the open loft door and back at the straw scattered on the floor.

How was it that I got up on the rafters earlier? And how did I get back down to the floor? I forgot why I was alone. I never played in the hayloft alone, but no one else was in the haymow now.

I thought hard and remembered that I had climbed up the ladder with my Dad close behind me and Preacher Pedermeier behind him. When we reached the hayloft, Daddy rolled me over and over on top of the wheat straw and tickled me. I giggled. Daddy and the preacher laughed too. I laughed so hard that Daddy stopped tickling and picked me up...and then. I couldn't remember what happened then. Next thing I knew I was on the rafters with the sparrows.

A gust of Kansas wind ripped through the open loft door sending a chill through me. Goose bumps popped up between the red blotches. I wanted to scramble to my feet and run, but I was shivering too much. It was so cold, I wished someone would come and wrap their arms around me to keep me warm. Maybe the birds would help me. With my eyes squeezed tight, I wished myself back up with my bird friends and waited. When I opened my eyes I was still on the floor.

The big square hole in the floor wasn't far away, the one where the ladder came up from the milk barn. Because my legs felt wobbly when I tried to stand, I crawled to the opening. With stubby fingers squeezed over the side board, I reached down the ladder with one foot until my tippy toes touched the next rung. Carefully I moved down another rung and then another holding tight to the wooden ladder in spite of splinters piercing my fingers.

Finally my feet felt the solid cement floor of the milk barn. My legs were steadier after climbing down the ladder, and I skittered past the horse stall towards the door to the farmyard.

The scent of ground oats wafted up from a manger and I heard the whinny of my Shetland pony, Rex. But I couldn't pet him; I couldn't even call to him because gunk clogged in my throat. Tabby, the mother barn cat meowed for her kittens and scurried to keep them safe from my footsteps.

Further down the hall I neared the separator room and smelled Daddy's cigarette smoke. Slipping quietly past the half-closed door, I caught a glimpse of the men. The preacher stood a head taller than Daddy. Dressed all in black with a big felt hat pulled down to his eyes he looked like a giant black monster.

Daddy only wore hats like that in pictures. Farmers wore striped denim caps that matched their overalls; ones that could be washed and starched and stretched over a pan turned upside down. Preacher Pedermeier never wore striped overalls; maybe he didn't have a striped barn hat either.

The men were laughing. Preacher Pedermeier sounded gruff, not gentle like when he preached on Sunday. "Little girls are like kittens, you know. They don't remember anything."

I wondered why the preacher was talking to my Dad about cats. Daddy didn't even like cats. A few days ago he said we had too many kittens and put some in gunny sacks with rocks and dropped them into the horse tank. That made me sad.

Outside the barn I ran fast as I could past the windmill and the car garage to the black walnut tree by the smokehouse. Hidden by the tree trunk, I stopped to catch my breath. Above me fluffy clouds rolled across the blue sky. The rainbow was gone.

Peeking beyond the tree, I spotted the open door of the hen house. That meant Mama must be gathering eggs, which only took a few minutes. Slipping past the smokehouse and the wooden gate to our little yard, I hurried towards the house hoping Mama wouldn't see me.

I wanted to sneak into my favorite hiding place, the little cupboard under the chimney. Snuggled inside the cupboard I'd be warm and the gooey stuff between my legs could dry.

But Mother reached the porch as the screen door slammed behind me. Crouched between the coal oil stove and the chimney cupboard, I heard her call, "Joyce, come here right now!"

Slowly I moved towards her. One look at her face told me I would never make it into the chimney cupboard. "I'm cold, very cold," came out of me in a whispery voice.

It didn't matter. Mother wasn't listening. She set the egg bucket down and marched across the kitchen towards the big rectangular sink where she gave me spit baths. With Mama's swift strokes on the pump handle, cold cistern water poured into the round enamel wash basin.

I struggled to speak louder when she reached for the jug of cleaner. "Please Mommy, no. Not Clorox. It burns my eyes and nose. It hurts me down there."

"Hush" she said as she grabbed my arms. I struggled but I couldn't escape her grip. She lifted me into the big white sink and dropped me into the basin.

My nose burned. I squeezed my eyes shut.

"Please Mama, no. Don't clean me up. I'm not dirty."

You can't wait for inspiration.
You have to go after it with a club.

Jack London

Jeanne Marsh

Born in Montgomery, Alabama, Jeanne Marsh grew up in the suburbs of Atlanta. She attended Auburn University, earning a BA degree in English. After graduation she accompanied her new husband, an electrical engineer and Air Force second lieutenant, to Vandenberg AFB, California, the morning after their wedding, and left her ancestral South for good. The military lifestyle suited her, as interesting transfers followed: historic Boston; picturesque Seattle; the high desert of California; a short stint in Norfolk; heartland Wichita; the southwestern melting pot of Albuquerque; and a final assignment to Colorado Springs. She and husband Brian have lived in the Pikes Peak area since 1986. Over their 48 years of marriage, the family circle expanded with the addition of two sons, Alan and Philip, and a daughter, Melinda. They and granddaughters Georgia and Gianna are the impetus for the memoir entries in this section.

With an MAT Degree in English from Salem State College in Massachusetts, Jeanne enjoyed a rich, though not enriching, career teaching English Language Arts, Reading, and Literature in multiple community colleges, before the family settled in Colorado. After ten years in Academy D20 public schools, she earned an MLS and spent the last years of her teaching career in the Fountain-Ft. Carson school district as an elementary school librarian, the teaching world's most satisfying occupation. She retired in 2003, joined AAUW and became a member of the nascent writers group when it formed in 2012.

The Little House

The little house sits on a couple of pine-dotted acres of amber clay Alabama countryside, next to an open gravel pit long out of production but never reclaimed to nature. Its exterior covered in tarpaper shingles, the homestead rests solidly on an open, raised foundation, harboring in the sheltering dark recesses of its crawl space a procession of animal life, from stray dogs and litters of kittens to the occasional black and white striped "woods pussy."

A swarm of hardworking honeybees hover in and around the two giant hydrangea bushes flanking the four concrete steps (recent additions, along with the metal handrail) leading to the front porch. Welcoming friends and family alike, a wooden swing sways in the moist, warm southern breeze, while two well-worn rocking chairs creak and beckon. A lazy hum from the wasp nest under the eve blends with the call of the mockingbird on a branch of the nearby crabapple tree, while the fragrance of freshly baked biscuits floats through the open kitchen window.

It's summer vacation finally, and my sister and I are staying with Maw and Paw (our maternal grandparents) for a week in the country. This year I'm a big girl; I won't cry and chase after the car when Mother and Daddy get ready to leave. Last year I was a silly little girl, and I'm embarrassed at the memory. This year Diane and I will lie under the sticky sheets on muggy summer nights, and through the open window we'll watch the lightning bugs flickering nearby, while heat lightning dances across the distant horizon.

Tomorrow we'll go to visit Becky and Bill, our summertime friends who live just down the dusty road. We'll play in the woods above the abandoned gravel pit, pretending to belong to the Cherokee or Creek people who inhabited this land when our ancestors still lived across the Atlantic. We'll construct bows and arrows from supple pine tree branches, and war clubs from stones and sturdier sticks of wood, held together with the long blades of grass growing at the edge of the trees. The campfires we make will be make-believe, only because we can't figure out how to twirl the fire sticks so that they send off sparks to catch the Spanish moss we've gathered.

As the long twilight descends, we'll go back to the little house for homemade pot roast and mashed potatoes; field corn, tomatoes and beans fresh from the garden; and those lighter-than-air biscuits only my grandmother can make. When the radio is turned off and we've taken "monkey baths" to freshen ourselves before bedtime, we'll snuggle up together on the big double bed beside the open window and dream sweet summertime dreams.

Comet and Cupid

It was a two-toned green and white pedal-brake, single-speed beauty of a bike, which my dad had secretly reconditioned in our basement as my special Christmas present in 1956. The white comet emblazoned on the chain guard made naming my steed a no-brainer. Comet was to carry me for the next few years from childhood to adolescence.

Encouraged by my uncle, who had recently moved to Atlanta to begin working with Delta, my dad had just been hired by the up-and-coming Atlanta-based airline. We bought a house on Myrtle Street in College Park, Georgia, two doors down from my mother's brother. Our little post-WWII bungalow sat in a neat row of identical two-bedroom, one-bath homes located two blocks from the chain-link fence marking the boundary of the Atlanta airport.

Our almost-daily bike rides took us neighborhood kids there to watch the new prop jets rev their engines before takeoff. Jim, my age, who lived across the street, and my younger cousin Susan and her friend Andy, were my riding partners. We would fly down "airport hill" to Myrtle Street, barely slowing down enough to make the sharp turn without a skid and disastrous plunge into the overgrown creek beyond the corner.

At other times the brambly thicket along the creek beckoned us to make-believe that we were in deepest Amazonian rain forest. The long trailing vines almost looked strong enough to swing on, though I don't remember ever trying. In those days summertime stretched endlessly, it seemed. After supper, when the lightning bugs were out, we kids collected them in canning jars with icepick-punched lids, and then we played hide and seek in the soft southern evenings until our parents called us in to bed.

All that, of course, was before that fateful Valentine's Day when Jim gave me my first box of candy, and I realized that boys were good for something besides bike racing and exploring muddy shallows for crawdads. It was probably his mother's idea, but the unexpected gesture still gave me a thrill I'll never forget. Nothing really changed in my life that day, but my teenage years were on the horizon, and Cupid would soon replace Comet.

Pretty Face

She was a fluffy grey tabby, not yet a year old, when she first entered our extended family. My sister was looking for a cat to keep our elderly parents company, so she called her vet to see whether he could help. Dr. Gingles, a family friend, had just been told by a client to euthanize the young cat, because she was mean. The doctor knew his cats—and his people. The kitten appeared perfectly healthy but traumatized and anti-social. Mean was not a word he could apply—at least, not to the cat. When my sister called, he was all too glad to offer her the little creature.

My dad had recently been diagnosed with Alzheimer's, and we knew my mom would need all the moral support she could get in the coming months and years. She had always had a soft spot for helpless animals, so Diane rescued the kitten and gave her as a gift to my parents.

Both Ben and Georgia were immediately in love with the vulnerable, shy youngster, and Daddy named her Pretty Face. Months went by and her timidity gave way to trust. She became attached to our parents, and they doted on her. She was gentle and loving toward them, but became terrified and hid whenever anyone else visited.

All too soon, it became necessary for my dad to move to a nursing facility. Mother wanted to be close to him, so she took a small apartment in a nearby senior living facility. Unfortunately, they did not allow pets. So my sister and her husband Jim made a home for Pretty Face. Their tomcat Garfield must have sensed her neediness, because he finally accepted her presence as part of the family. She in turn became very attached to him, and a stealthy camera several times caught the two of them curled up together. Gradually, Pretty Face came out of her shell as she began to feel safe in her new home and trust her new people. Jim was particularly smitten with her gentle squeaks and frequent soft purring. His lap was her favorite spot, and he claimed he owed his very healthy blood pressure to her lap habit. He renamed her simply Gray Cat, and she didn't seem to mind. As she gained confidence, she even welcomed visitors, and often curled up beside them when they shared her couch.

Years passed, and Pretty Face was thirteen, the sweetest, calmest and most loving cat I've ever known. Then disaster struck my sister's home in Gulfport, MS, in the form of Hurricane Katrina. Their lovely home on Bayou Bernard was destroyed in the wind and tidal surge.

Many previous evacuations had left them somewhat complacent; when they left the house in the face of the imminent storm, they expected to return in a couple of days, as usual. So they left plenty of food and water for Pretty Face on the upstairs bathroom countertop and shut her into the house when they left to head inland.

The knowledge that their home and most of their belongings were gone was a huge psychological blow, but the worst fear was that Pretty Face had perished in the storm. As soon as he could navigate the devastated roads, Jim returned to the destruction of their home. The structure was twisted on its foundation, there was a boat dock shoved through the plate glass of their bedroom window, the roof was gone, and the receding flood waters had strewn their belongings over the lawn and driveway.

Risking his own life, Jim laid a ladder against the front of the house to the front door, as the stairs were gone. Pretty Face met him at the door, clearly weak and traumatized, but unhurt. During the worst of the storm she had evidently climbed into the dining room closet, a refuge which protected her (and incidentally, Diane's fine china).

Pretty Face lived with her family for seven more years before succumbing to the inevitable health problems of old age. When she was twenty, Jim and Diane lost her, but that graceful, loving creature who endured so much will long be remembered by all of us who so admired her chutzpah.

Nifty

Pretty Nifty was her name. Better known as Nifty, she was 16-1/2 hands at the withers and a bundle of excitable muscle, ready to jump any fence or take off across the empty pasture at full gallop the instant she felt a give on the reins. As a novice rider and first-time owner, I didn't realize that she was too much horse for me.

She wasn't beautiful; half Morgan, half question mark, she probably was part Clydesdale, judging from her size, her markings, the feathers on her fetlocks, and her heavy Roman-nosed face. Never mind all that—I loved her. I loved the way my hands tugged against her insistent mouth and the way my heart leapt into my throat when I finally let her take the bit into her teeth; the way the winter wind bit into my face as her mane whipped into my eyes and I gave up control, trusting to her sure-footed confidence and (less so) to my ability to stick to the saddle.

Winter was breathtakingly beautiful in the northeastern countryside, away from the noise and bustle of the city. As my friends and I rode across the fallow fields, the plowed rows of frostbitten earth spewed upwards toward the icy blue sky. Of course, autumn and spring brought the most moderate riding weather, as summers were hot and humid. But those lazy summer days also lured our small band of lady equestriennes to the banks of the nearby lake, where we would ground-tie the horses to graze and sit on the soft grass drinking Cold Duck.

I realized that right then I might very well be experiencing the best life could offer. As a young Air Force officer's wife, I was living in Bedford, Massachusetts, a bucolic and historic rural town near Boston. With no children, my graduate school studies left time for leisure. The opportunity to fulfill my lifelong dream of owning a horse was too much to resist. Even now I look back with gratitude to the generosity of the retired Lt. Colonel's wife, my riding instructor—$2.00 lesson, horse included—and the indulgence of my husband to encourage my hobby. It was the best of times, and though many years have passed, those golden days remain a memory I cherish.

Aviators of Woodmen Valley

Scattered composite sandstone pillars, reminders and remnants of a very different ancient landscape, the "hoodoos" stand sentinel over a quiet, secluded valley tucked away just beyond the northwest boundary of Colorado Springs. It is early July. Nestled in the protective foliage of the Gambel oak clusters and flitting through the claw-like lower branches of the Ponderosa pines, the hummingbirds have returned to Woodmen Valley.

Tiny metallic green bodies, accented with red and white collars, four male hummers buzz about the feeders suspended from our pergola. The little kamikaze flyers, though sated by wildflower nectar, still defend their territory from intruders. No sooner does one dip a long, slim beak into the plastic flowers guarding the artificial nectar, than another swoops to the attack. The Air Force Thunderbirds, which periodically perform over the Valley during football season and at Academy graduation, could probably learn from the fearless tactics of these avian dogfights.

The Past

The Past is a work of art, free of irrelevancies and loose ends.

–Max Beerbohm

...or as my friend Marge once commented, "We twist it to suit ourselves."

We always remember the highlights: graduations, weddings, births of children and grandchildren, special vacations or holiday events. The rest of personal history tends to morph into vague impressions or attitudes. Like a work of art, the interpretation is always left to the observer, and sometimes the interpretation changes over time, as experiences and attitudes develop more complex nuances.

As a child when I saw my first Van Gogh painting, the globby brush strokes and blended colors reminded me of my paint-by-numbers kit. Though I liked the effect, I saw nothing of depth in works like *Starry Night*. Yet with my teenage angst came an understanding of the emotional turmoil which must have inspired such intense artistic expression.

When I was young in the South, our family employed several African-American housecleaners from time to time to help my working mother. I never thought much about their personal lives, other than to notice occasional offensive body odors that assailed my "delicate sensibilities." Only when I was an adult, with the civil rights battles behind us and the awareness of racial inequalities pricking my conscience, did I realize that the reason those hardworking, devoted ladies did not bathe daily was because they had no running water or indoor bathrooms in their homes.

Just by living beyond an event, our perceptions change. We rationalize, synthesize and fit our experiences into the emerging fabric of life, making the pieces fit as neatly as possible into our present world view, whatever that may be. The past, then, is not a static, accomplished set of facts which we remember. Instead, it is an ever-changing kaleidoscope of shifting impressions. How we interpret the past depends on our evolving attitudes, shaped by experience and reason, but also by our current emotional state of mind. The past is as fluid as a river of dreams, flowing into consciousness as tributaries flow into the sea.

What Is Poetry?

Is poetry merely a clever juxtaposition of words and rhyme, or a
brilliant flash of truth in symbols and metaphors?

Is poetry a pure truth exposed finally when all extra verbiage is stripped
away?

Is poetry raw emotion thrust forth from an anguished or ebullient soul?
Why do options have to come in threes before the solution is revealed?

Scribbles

Scribbles on white
With lines to give form
No thought to rhythm or balance
     Or any such convention
Poetry is what comes when the mind is open
     Not still

Silence

Silence never happens in life
While life goes on there is no peace
Thoughts are noisy, intruding on calm
The sound of silence is a myth

Broken

Thoughts are fragile, inspiration in spurts
Distractions are many, invading consciousness
No chance for completion of written images
When not even a concept emerges in full

The Nature of Music

When sound forms itself into music, the chords strike soul and body. Let notes pour forth in rivers of melody or conflicting discordant strains, in mellow smoothness or shivery waves of violent contrast, and a song is born. Hearts and minds awake to rhythm, tone and meter. Words may enrich-but not necessarily-the pitch and roll of sound controlled by a vision, an impression, or expression of emotion: serenity/upheaval; hope/despair; devotion/separation; joy/depression. Music is life lived in common, sounds reflecting the breadth of shared human experience. The inspiration of the musician emerges from the primitive urge of humankind for self-expression, yet also emanates from a mysterious spiritual source. And the soul of the listener responds.

Dixie Gordon

I was born in Mesa, Arizona, to Robert and Phyllis Dale from Holt and Richmond, Missouri. My brother, Robert Vest Dale, was five at the time and we were the perfect family of four. Because my father was in the U.S. Air Force, we moved every two years. From Arizona we moved to San Angelo, Texas, Yakota, Japan, Jefferson City, Missouri, St. Paul, Minnesota, Richfield, Minnesota, Grandview, Missouri, Manila, Philippines, Tachikawa, Japan, and landed in San Antonio, Texas, before I went off to college at Oklahoma State University. After eight years I graduated with a teaching degree in Business Education while working and supporting my family of three. When my daughter Dana was born, I worked at home managing apartments. When I moved to Oklahoma City, I worked in property management, divorced and remarried. My current mate of 39 years and I combined two families and raised his three sons and my daughter. All grown, educated, with families of their own, they have blessed us with six grandchildren. They are great citizens, great parents, good people, and we could ask for nothing more. Upon retirement seven years ago, we moved from Oklahoma City to Colorado Springs, Colorado. During my career, I was able to travel the world, visiting almost every continent and most countries. Life has exceeded my expectations; I have great memories and experiences to write about.

Life's Most Important Things

How fortunate we were to have loving, concerned parents who gave us our Wings to Fly!

Their Missouri Roots provided some of the best values for us to live by. Honest, Trustworthy, Kind, Giving, Appreciative, Respectful, Dependable, are only a few.

There are many choices "You" must carefully make and overcome adversity to see your way through.

It was a happy time with lots of changes to endure: moving every two years made adjustments necessary and at times we were not so sure.

My brother and I have no regrets and our times together now are very dear; we only wish our parents were here so we could share with them how great they were.

Patriotism was a big part of our lives you know; my dad kissed the ground when we returned from living abroad so it literally showed.

We both held jobs from being teens as we knew money was scarce; frugality was a way of means.

Education was stressed. There was no other choice you know; not Where but When to college you must go.

We hunted, we fished, traveled near and far; all together we shared dinner each and every night.

It was Nature, Family, Friends, and Fun. We minded them as we only thought that was right.

Arizona, Texas, Japan, Missouri, Minnesota, Missouri again, Philippine Islands, Japan and Texas to End!!! Always special were family and friends.

No pianos. No pets. That was too much to move about. Times always changing and activities of shared love we shout.

WE COULD ASK FOR NOTHING MORE.

June Hallenbeck

June was born in Pontiac, Michigan, and moved to Flint while she was still an infant. When she was eight, her family moved to the near-by town of Grand Blanc, where her father had built a house on forty country acres. She was proficient in academics, and was at the top of her high school class. At the University of Michigan she received a B.S. in Medical Technology. After graduating and passing the rigid board exams, she worked as a Medical Technologist in hospital laboratories and in private clinics. She married Ken, her college sweetheart, and they moved to Monterey, California, for his military service. They later settled in Fort Wayne, Indiana, where they started their family. After 21 years in Indiana, Ken took a position as curator of the American Numismatic Association's money museum in Colorado Springs. Five years later while continuing to raise the family,

June helped Ken establish the Hallenbeck Coin Gallery, which has become the area's premier numismatic business.

When June was in her early 50s, she entered the graduate engineering program at University of Colorado at Colorado Springs to earn her Master of Science degree in Computer Science. She then worked for eleven years as a software engineer, helping develop and test government programs in Cheyenne Mountain.

In retirement, June and Ken enjoy visiting their four children and fourteen grandchildren residing in four states. They also frequently indulge in their passion for foreign and domestic travel, having visited dozens of exotic countries throughout of the world, as well as wide-ranging destinations within the United States.

If My Life Were a Quilt

Well, my life actually IS a quilt—a beautiful combination of a hand-made and machine-quilted wall-hanging that I look at every morning as I lay in bed before I get up.

It consists of thirty blocks containing the most important persons and stages of my life, all quilted together with multi-hued fabrics in every color of the rainbow.

"Where did you get this quilt?" you ask. I say, "It is a beautiful and extremely meaningful gift from my family for my seventieth birthday, assembled by Diane, my oldest son's wife." "What is in the thirty blocks?" you ask. "Pictures and writings," I say. "Pictures from my earliest and current days—captured as photos and digitally reproduced on the individual fabric squares."

There is a picture of me as an infant, superimposed on a picture of my parents. And there is a picture of me in my cap and gown graduating from college.

Then there is a picture of my husband Ken and me cutting the cake at our wedding, with a rather unsentimental message from Ken in his typical male style.

"Did you really look like that?" you ask. "We hardly recognize you now." "Forty-seven years does make a difference," I say, "but that was really the two of us in 1955."

What other things are captured in that quilt? Well, there is a picture of me with my two siblings—my brother Dick and my sister Shirley. Both Dick and Shirley have written greetings on their own squares.

Next we have a picture of Ken and me with our first child—a son just a few months old. Then there is a photo of our family growing up—three boys and a girl with our daughter clinging to my arm. It was taken in front of Ken's parents' home at the funeral of Ken's father, a beautiful picture that brings back both wonderful and sad memories.

In the corners of the quilt are wedding pictures of each of our four children (Kevin, Tom, Scott and Sheri.) There are pictures of each of the three families that had children at the time the quilt was made and greetings from all. And last but not least are handprints of each grandchild (12 at that time) embroidered with their name, each on a separate block.

All of these squares were quilted together by my daughter-in-law, gathered from all the family members and filled with love. How fitting that the quilt contains a multitude of colors, so very bright and cheerful. What a great feeling I get each morning, looking at all the blessings in my quilt of life!

Africa

Out the plane's window, the river flows
around and around islands, small and large.
An animal moves, and then many more—
Look, elephants and giraffes on the run!
On a small clearing the plane lands and
a Land Rover appears from the bushes—
but where did the elephants go?

Now a boat, then a camp, the staff welcoming us
with cool, wet towels and refreshing drinks.
A tent along the shore—two cots,
a toilet like a throne on a hill,
a bucket of water for a shower.
A campfire with seats, some wine, beer and toasts,
and a promise of elephants to come.

At daybreak, a boat, then Land Rovers appear.
What will we see?
A giraffe, then another—and elephants galore.
A huge male lion, right on the road—"Don't move,"
the driver tells us, "Be quiet"—we freeze.
Lion walks, we follow. He roars, lies down under a tree.
All's quiet again, spot marked for others to see.
And now there are hippos and elephants, more.

Night falls and the campfire is lit. Tents beckon.
Cots call and frogs croak in the river.
Wake up! Wake up! Look outside!
Ten feet from the tent an elephant walks.

This is what we came to Africa to see!

Travel Poem

Myanmar

Whir of motor as our boat is freed from sandbar.
Monsoons will come and river will rise.
Peanuts and beans will be harvested, then drown.
People living on shore will move to higher ground.
Monsoons will end and river level will drop.
The people come back, planting peanuts and beans,
moving homes back to the sandbar.
Another season has passed on the Irrawaddy River.

The land of pagodas—five million we are told.
People are praying, feet are bare.
Do you know the day of the week you were born?
You must pour water on your Buddha.
Gold leaf for sale, good karma if you
paste yours on a pagoda, stupa, temple, Buddha.
Ring a gong—good karma for you
and for all who hear it.
People are praying, feet are bare.

June Hallenbeck

Kenya and Tanzania

Into the Masai Mara we fly.
Warriors jump high to greet us.
Bad monkey—leave my food alone!
He scampers to the top of the tent with a
Mouthful.
In the Ngorongoro Crater
The lion roars: "I'm guarding this
Cape buffalo carcass for my family.
Keep back, you hyenas and jackals and vultures!
Your time will come."

It's February and all the wildebeest
have given birth in the Serengeti.
The calves stay close to mamas.
Many thousands of them are safe from
Predators.
A few are eaten.
The laws of Nature prevail.

Last Words

She traveled the world
from A (Amsterdam) to Z (Zimbabwe).

And still she traveled more
with husband Ken and children four.

Seeing her fourteen grandchildren run—
and grow they did to young adults—
so proud they made her every one!

She worked, she played,
she cooked and prayed.

And now the time has come to travel on,
and say goodbye to the setting sun.

What lies ahead she now will find
and thanks her friends and all mankind.

Joyce Calamia

Joyce is a Colorado Girl. Most of her education took place in Denver. She attended Denver Public Schools and was granted an undergraduate degree from the University of Denver. She also earned a Master's degree from UCLA.

The pride of her life is her two beautiful, brilliant daughters and her wonderful, intelligent husband.

Joyce taught in Colorado's Jefferson County School District for 36 years. She had a wonderful and rewarding career.

Writing has been a special love of hers since she was in elementary school. She first joined a writing group 17 years ago. Joyce started Word Weavers a small writing group eight years ago, belongs to a journaling group and is delighted to be a member of Women Who Write.

The Dance Recital

My oldest daughter Becky was five years old when she started dancing lessons at Dan Shannon's School of Dance. Becky's father was six foot five and Becky was already showing signs of taking after him. I wanted her to learn to stand tall and be proud of her height. Becky excelled at dancing and loved her lessons. In fact when she graduated from high school she opened her own dancing school in the basement of our house.

But this story isn't about Becky, it is about Melissa, Becky's little sister. Becky was six years old when Melissa was born. From the time Melissa was two month's old she went with Becky and me for Becky's lessons.

Dan had a strict policy that parents were to stay in the waiting room during the class until the last five minutes when we could go into the studio and watch what our little darlings learned. The door between the waiting room and the studio was tightly closed so any snoopy parents could not sneak a peek.

Melissa was just barely two years old and she would stand by my chair during parent visiting time and try to imitate the children in the class dancing. If anybody would accidentally leave the door open during class she would stand in the doorway and "dance" with the class. By the time she was three all she could talk about was when she would take dancing lessons. At the end of every class she would look hopefully up at Dan and ask. "When can I take dancing lessons?" Dan would answer patiently, "When you are four." With a sigh she would look at him with big brown eyes turn, and slowly walk away.

Dan began keeping the waiting room door open when we were there. Melissa would stretch, and kick and plié and pirouette while hanging onto the side of the doorway. Early on Melissa decided on just what outfit she would wear to dancing school. She had an old pair of pink stretch tights, size 18 months, she wore under dresses from the time she was about one and a half years old. These became her dancing school tights. She didn't really care what her top looked like, she was determined she was going to wear these tights.

Meanwhile the pink tights were not getting any newer or bigger and Melissa was not getting smaller. The tights finally reached the limit of their stretch. The gap between the bottom or the shirt she was wearing and where the top of the tights reached didn't bother Melissa, this was her dancing school outfit and this was what she was going to wear to dancing school.

Melissa's fourth birthday finally rolled around. Not too soon for Melissa nor the pink tights. Melissa was thrilled. I was glad too, because I had the distinct feeling the other parents were thinking about taking up a collection to buy the child some new tights. Actually Melissa had a drawer full of tights that fit her, but they were not pink. I had combed the city looking for bigger pink tights. They were not to be found.

The day of her first dancing class Melissa, head held high, wore the official class outfit: black leotards and black tights. She carried her new tap shoes, complete with jingle taps, and new pink practice ballet slippers in a new carrying case decorated with a beautiful ballet dancer. When we got to dancing school she pranced straight through the waiting room and right into the classroom where she belonged.

You are probably wondering by now, Is she ever going to get to the dance recital? I will get to that, I promise you, but first I want to build up a little sympathy. For me.

The year went smoothly. Dance classes went wonderfully. Becky was now in two classes and with the one Melissa was in I was at dancing school three times a week. It did give me a time to grade papers.

At Christmas time small groups of children went to different nursing homes and hospitals around town to entertain. Melissa and her class danced and sang to "Me and My Teddy Bear." Melissa sang loud and didn't miss a beat. She loved wearing a costume, a little bit of makeup and performing in front of people and audiences.

Spring was approaching and it was time to prepare for the BIG Annual Spring Recital. Melissa's class was performing to "Be My Little Baby Bumble Bee - Buzz Around, Buzz Around." Their costume was a black leotard and tights with yellow bands of cloth sewn horizontally around the body of the leotard. One of the mother's and I made twenty little head pieces with bee antennas formed out of fat pipe cleaners.

The recital was held in a high school with a large auditorium. My husband was in charge of the lighting or sound or some technical thing. My job was to stay in a classroom with two other mothers and keep twenty four year olds entertained, quiet, and neat while the wiggly worms waited for their turn to perform. We were to walk them to the back stage and have them wait quietly in the wings at the beginning of the act before them. In this case it was Becky's solo performance.

Dress rehearsal went smoothly. Melissa's class tapped out on stage in order, danced and stole the show as four year olds were apt to do. Well, you know what is said about dress rehearsals...

The morning of recital day two little girls one ten and the other four, with strangely made up faces were flying high. Costumes gathered, tap shoes collected, books and games to entertain during the waiting packed. We drove by and picked up grandparents and went on our merry way across town to the high school. I leaned back in the passenger's seat and sighed a sigh of relief. Everything was perfect. The only tight spot that needed to be choreographed perfectly was between Becky's solo and helping her change in time for her class dance. At rehearsal it went off just fine. Not to worry.

Melissa's class was waiting quietly in the wings. The other mothers and I were busy making last minute adjustments to bumble bee costumes. I was also watching Becky dancing on stage in her beautiful new white satin costume I made. Becky was near the end of her dance when I felt a tug at my skirt and there was Melissa saying, "I'm not going to do it."

"What aren't you going to do?" I asked.

"I am not going out there and dance."

"Now, Melissa," I began, "your grandparents are out there waiting to watch you dance..." As I was talking I made a tactical mistake. I hunkered down to be on eye level with the child. Two arms caught me in a strangle hold around my neck and two legs crushed me around the middle.

Applause roared from the audience and I caught a glimpse of Becky taking her bows. Before I could begin to unclamp body parts from around my body I heard Becky wail behind me, "Mom, I have a bloody nose!"

I stood up and turned around quickly as I could considering my four year old burden. Sure enough there was Becky with blood streaming from her nose. As nineteen bumblebees tapped their way onto the stage to bumblebee music some kind soul handed me a handful of Kleenex since I couldn't get to my skirt pocket because of—you know who.

We got the nose bleed and the crying stopped. Becky and I along with my Siamese twin rushed to the dressing room, changed costumes, repaired the tear-stained makeup and got back to the wings just as the entrance music for Becky's class was started.

I peeled a happy Melissa from the front of me. As I stood there holding her hand and watching the ten years olds go perfectly through their routine I wondered why nobody had invented retroactive birth control.

Tiny Pieces of Promises

Tiny pieces of promises how important or insignificant they can be.
I think I can live the rest of my life without them, considering how
empty yours are.
You call, you write and I hear the same insincere words over again.
The problem is I know you too well.

At one time I believed these grandiose overtures of a bright and
beautiful future.
The road ahead was paved with golden bricks and diamonds sparkling
like the stars.
An earthbound Milky Way possibly?
I looked at you with cow brown eyes absorbing all the crap you were
dishing out.
But that was another me.
A me that will never be found again. I know this, but you have no
clue.

I like this wiser me.
The me who discovered truer rainbows.
Rainbows that float across the skies of my mind and
deliver a pot of gold every time.
This me dances with the universe, waltzes with butterflies, tangos
with tigers,
jitterbugs with the future.
This me may last a life time.

Joyce Calamia

The cataracts of naiveté have been laser-rayed away and I no longer
need your
promises, because they are worthless.
The road with you was not golden bricks but a morass of mud
that tried to suck me down with every step.
The diamonds you promised became tears and sorrow.

Now you're here again, same smile, same warm eyes,
same tiny pieces of promises,
but this time I'm not buying.

The Piano Lessons

Before she started taking piano lessons she felt so disconnected, so worthless, so betrayed. Her husband, Sam, the rat, left her after 20 years of marriage. He placed a note on the living room mantle saying he was flying off to Australia with that redhead who sold admission tickets at Tinseltown. Deep down, she wasn't really surprised.

She and Sam, the rat, owned a very successful business that supplied movie theaters everything they needed for their concession stands. They supplied the food, beverages and the equipment that dispensed these items. The business also supplied 24-hour maintenance for this equipment.

She and Sam put in 60-hour work weeks until the business was established. At least she put in 60 hours. When he wasn't playing golf, Sam would walk around the office and warehouse with a bewildered look on his face. She did her best to keep him out of the way of their employees. Playing golf was what Sam really did best. At least that was what she thought before she realized that Sam must have had some other talents she didn't know about.

She should have suspected something when he started coming home late and going out evenings on service calls. They had a service staff for that, but Sam said that these were special problems that only he could take care of. At last Sam was becoming interesting in the business she told herself.

Sam asked that she have her lawyer deposit one million dollars into the Australian account he sat up and the business was all hers. He and Red were going to start a kangaroo ranch. Her lawyer laughed when he heard Sam's demands, and said, "Sam really didn't know much about the business, did he?"

The lawyer wasted no time contacting a legal firm in Australia and as quickly as possible the equipment firm and all its assets were signed over to her while one million dollars was deposited in Sam's new bank account. Sam had his new life and she was left with a broken heart and a business that was worth many millions of dollars.

After weeks of ranting, raving and crying her eyes out she got out of bed one morning, threw all of Sam's belongings into a dumpster. She sold her wedding rings and tossed all of the wedding china across the kitchen, smashing it into hundreds of pieces. She felt a lot better after all that exercise.

During her mourning period she lost a lot of weight so she checked into the most expensive spa she could find for six weeks and enjoyed a complete makeover. When she got home she hired a personal trainer. She looked great!

She began going to the country club functions and jumped into the single life with glee. Her social calendar was full and the phone rang constantly with calls from friends. It wasn't long before she forgot all about Sam. Soon she was wondering about getting a hobby or taking up some new activity to broaden her mind and her horizons.

An old friend invited her to a dinner party and she met the friend's piano teacher. He was not only an extremely talented pianist, he was buff and breathtakingly handsome. Learning to play the piano was just what she needed to keep her mind active.

The piano teacher came to her home twice, sometimes three times a week. The lessons were wonderful and she learned quickly. She looked forward to each lesson with delightful anticipation. One afternoon as she stood in her front doorway with a contented smile on her face, waving as the piano teacher drove away, she thought to herself, *Someday, I'm really going to have to buy a piano.*

I was a late bloomer.
But anyone who blooms at all, ever, is very lucky.

Sharon Olds

Joann Oh

I am who I am because of:

- my childhood in St. Louis with my loving, overprotective (so I thought at the time) parents and my younger brother-buddy;
- my fun neighborhood of 26 kids;
- my large, caring German family;
- my challenging schools with much-loved classes but social barriers;
- the gifts of my beloved, less-demanding college: knowledge and a ticket to graduate school but also Han Soo, my husband of 51 years, and many lifelong friends;
- my marriage in 1964 to Han Soo from South Korea that had to be in Illinois because of Missouri's anti-miscegenation law;
- my enjoyable position as an associate professor with tenure at Sinclair Community College in Dayton for eight years B.C. (Before Children);

- our move with two small children to Wisconsin, where we knew no one but found warm friendships;

- my 22 years of meaningful classes in the University of Wisconsin system teaching English as a Second Language (ESL) at a technical college to Hmong adults newly arrived from refugee camps and Freshman Composition and multicultural Modern American Literature at UW-Oshkosh.

- our fascinating trips across the U.S.A. and to Australia, New Zealand, China, Europe, and South Korea with nine visits to Han Soo's welcoming family;

- my husband, two daughters, two sons-in-law, and four young grandchildren, from whom I have learned many lessons, especially about love.

In 1999 Han Soo and I retired to Colorado Springs, the crossroads where we met and matched with new friends and a new way of life that has included many stimulating activities, such as writing for self-exploration, sharing, and FUN!

Joann Oh

Spring Green

Our silver Sienna was streaking along on I-70 heading east,
Heading east to Chillicothe, Missouri, northeast of Kansas City
To say farewell to Pete on this dim, dull day of March.

Dawn should have been breaking, but clouds blocked the sun
And shed just a few weak streams of light.
We drove on in enveloping morning mist.

We were really sailing along at over 75 miles an hour,
But we seemed to be just snailing along on that flat Kansas prairie,
On that gray graphite pencil-line of highway drawn ruler-straight.

We saw only gray skies and winter-seared fields of bleached-out
   cornstalks,
Gray grasses, brown dirt ridges with muddy puddles in between.
Scattered black cattle searched for something to eat.
Dead weed-balls tumbled drunkenly across our path.

The flat, straight road, the sunless sky, the surrounding wasteland
Weighed on our spirits, as did the thought of wonderful Pete, now gone,
And those he left behind: Lucy, his wife of 64 years,
Three children, six grandchildren, innumerable friends and relatives.

Suddenly, up in the air, out of the mist came dozens of three-armed monsters,
Metal blades flailing at what? Birds? Bugs? Oh, just the air!
The wind turned the turbines, and knives slashed through the air.

Down on the ground, ugly monsters marched out of the mist,
Pressing their metal arms down, up, down, deeply down and
Pumping up oil, black gold to feed our need for raw power and speed.

167

Where are we heading? What's left behind?
What can we give now to help our descendants
Live meaningful lives, be generous, be bold?

After forty-eight hours, our silver Sienna was sailing west on I-70,
Streaking along on that straight, flat road heading home to the mountains
After saying farewell to Pete and hugging those left behind.

Bright sun shone down on tan cornstalks glinting golden.
Emerald squares of winter wheat glowed green in the sunlight.
Black cattle grazed on green shoots, newborn calves at their sides.
Shiny machines produced power for our comfortable lives.

But something stronger than sunlight and shiny machines lifted our spirits.
Lucy and Pete planted seeds for the future.
Working themselves and gathering others,
Fund-raising, grant-writing, whatever it took,
They bent to the plow of civic improvement and raised up their harvest:
A wonderful Y and a beautiful church and a great public golf course,
Many Habitat houses, all fruits of their labor.
Lives in their town are immeasurably better for what they have done.

They planted more seeds in their children and grandchildren,
Who, with worldly success, now give back to the world.
Their intelligent giving, their caring for others
Touches futures of their children, our children too.

The world turns on its axis; the seasons wheel by.
At the end of dead winter, spring green is revealed.

Summer Fish: To Risk or Not to Risk

Several years ago, my husband and I explored the Big Island of Hawaii for two weeks in February. We played in the waves at white-sandy Hapuna Bay, waded in the Puna lagoons, visited the windy cliffs of South Point, walked the intriguing lava moonscape of Volcanoes National Park, saw the lovely waterfalls near Hilo, drove the 2000' drop to the black sand beach and wild horses of Waiapio, and took two boat tours to snorkel at the Capt. Cook Monument Marine Sanctuary.

When we returned in early May of 2013 after two months of 25 items every day on our to-do lists, we wanted relaxation for our minds and bodies. But we were faced with hot, humid weather not meant for sightseeing, fewer fish at the Captain Cook Monument Bay, and high surf warnings that made playing in the waves rather scary. What should we do to make this vacation special? We tried cooling off by snorkeling in various coves with many unsatisfactory fish-sightings.

Then we happened upon Beach #69. It was named after the number on a nearby telephone pole, which, strangely enough, is now #71. Beach #69 possessed many of our Beach Requirements. It was protected from the high surf and was close to the parking lot, which was not crowded because not many people know about it. It had a shower and a concrete house with toilets and changing room; it also had shade trees near the water for my husband, who is not as enthusiastic about snorkeling as I am. And it was very scenic with a long crescent of white sand beach and rough black lava rocks peeking out of the waves. It was also low cost—like $0.00. However, we saw no lifeguard, a beach requirement that my cousin, who has lived in Hawaii for 45 years, told me to demand of any place where I was in the water. Oh well, "You can't have everything!" as my mother used to say.

Secure in the belief that, "What happens in Hawaii stays in Hawaii," I never have a problem dressing for comfort and snorkel-ability rather than for sex appeal when I go into the water. With my swimming suit on, I slipped into my long-sleeved, faded blue REI sun block shirt, smeared waterproof sun-block onto my neck and the backs of my legs, and pulled on my slick black swimming cap, which prevented any hair from getting tangled in the strap of my mask and prevented any hair-gaps in the suction of the mask to my face. I wiped gunk onto my mask to keep it from fogging up and anchored it on my forehead. I sat on a large chunk of smooth white driftwood and pulled my blue flippers over the thick white ankle socks that cushioned my feet. I stood up. Pulling down my mask as I went, I lifted my flippered feet high to avoid getting tripped by incoming waves and sucking sand, and with about five flap-flap-flaps I was able to flop forward into two feet of clear aqua water.

One hard thrust of my flippers and…maybe ten large black fish with a brushstroke of orange on their sides and tails cruise right in front of me…a long yellow goatfish with drooping goatee swims by…small navy blue with orange spots puffer fish float around me…two gorgeous parrot fish, maybe 15 inches and 12 inches long, in pale pastels of aqua, pink, and yellow go about their business of gnawing seaweed off the lava rocks with their made-for-it buck teeth, large black rocks that hold lovely coral in decorative designs.

With the hot sun on my shirt-protected back, I relax and enjoy my god-like view of this totally different world: Several times I float over a green sea turtle with a shell two feet in diameter. Will he nip me? But he is very busy scraping seaweed off the rocks too. An eel colored strangely in pink with dark spots slithers from one black lava hole to another, and I am glad that I am far above him. Several flat bright yellow butterfly fish school by, and a whole squadron of small yellow with black stripes sergeant fish head off on a mission. A jaw-heavy grouper with wide, dark purple stripes lingers. Large, nearly-transparent white fish lazily drift by, and then more black fish, these with neon blue racing stripes along their spines, zip past. Tiny, colorful fish dart about; large, colorful fish calmly do tail-strokes. Finally, I spot my favorites, the *humuhumunukunukuapuaa*, the Hawaiian state fish with their tilted-back foreheads, black masks, and Mondrian-tattooed bodies. I am entranced, literally *in a trance*, as I float on the rising and falling swells, sometimes using my flippers to power to another intriguing spot.

Only very occasionally do I feel a prickle of anxiety as an intruder into this beautiful, seemingly perfect world; this is the dangerous ocean, after all. I have heard about the jellyfish whose sting can stop my heart, and I have seen the slashes on the legs of my husband and daughter from the whipping tentacles of a man o' war. I have seen pictures of shark-bitten surfboards and of the young woman who was a top surfer in Hawaii till a shark took her arm. I thrust down these dark thoughts, become intrigued with an incredibly graceful white, yellow, and black-striped angelfish, and let my feelings of being daring and adventurous in my old age buoy me up.

Finally, after my second snorkel-swim, the realization that I am tired and really must go in finally sinks into my inebriated brain. With mask and snorkel up, flippers and socks pulled off in the swells before the surf-break, I stride up to the beach feeling great, inspired, uplifted. A woman looking out to where I have just been, asks, "Did you see the reef shark?"

"Noooooo," I answer. "Where is it?"

"See those people pulling the little boy on the surfboard out to that big, black rock? They are going to show him the black-tipped reef shark that hangs out in a sea cave. He's about five feet long, but reef sharks don't attack people—usually!" I had floated leisurely by this cave in a big lava rock while being entranced by underwater beauty.

On the beach a lanky college student from Berkeley asks me about other snorkeling spots. I ask him whether he has seen the shark. Although he had been ready to leave, he cannot resist swimming out to see the shark. I beg him not to go because it will be my fault if he gets hurt. He goes anyway but strokes hastily back to tell me, "That shark was as big as me! He was moving around in the cave very restlessly. I swam back as fast as I could."

We came back to Beach #69 and snorkeled the next day. What risks are worth it? Some are.

A Fall Peak Experience

A fun fall hike...to a peak with a view...
near Jirisan, South Korea, yet! on a cool, crispy November day, yet!
with my husband Han Soo and Noella, our petite Korean guide—yes!,
We are packing water bottles, and Noella is carrying snacks—hooray!

Hiking poles--yes! Hiking shoes—yes! Layered clothing—yes!
a short drive to the trailhead—yes! A colorful, leaf-layered trail—yes!

And so we start climbing upward beside a hard-rushing stream.

Patterns appear: sunlit flashes on running water,
      gushing water forced between massive dark rocks,
      smooth-flowing water sliding over worn-silky stones.

We pause for photos. We have lots of time. We aren't going far.
      Or so we think!

More patterns appear: orange, red, golden leaves on trees and on trail,

rock steps, black blocks with white stripes,
  more rock steps, some flat, some lumpy-bumpy.

We climb upward and upward: Is the path steeper, or is it just me?

Hiking styles differ: Darling, pack-laden Noella climbs tirelessly;
  athletic but 80-year-old Han Soo climbs slowly and steadily;
  fairly fit I climb faster with periodic pauses for breath.

The rushing river inspires but then leaves us, curving to the left;
  we continue climbing straight up! and up! and UP!

Observations occur: Noella is 49 but looks 19. As a child, she walked
    over two of these mountains every day to school.
  Husband Han Soo is using his golf-toughened shoulders to hoist
    himself up, pressing on poles.
  I am thinking, "Why didn't I hike more in Colorado?" and
    "Where are the switchbacks?"

Upward, straight upward.

More questions appear: "Who made these amazing stone steps four
    feet across?"
  "Did they ever think of just digging out the stones?"
  "Did they ever think of making a sandy ramp instead of steps?"

Upward and onward.

We sit and rest. We take photos to excuse our need to catch our breath.
We look up at yet 50…more…steep…steps.
Noella encourages us, "After this steep bit the trail is much easier."

Still steeply upward and upward!

We look to the side at the drop down the valley; the angle we hike at is
      45 degrees.
Finally, finally, we lose those rock steps; the trail becomes earthy,
      Angling less sharply.
The trees open up; looking down gives us heart knowing how far we've
      come.

Not so steeply upward but still onward.

We meet friends—amazing kindness!
We eat snacks—amazing tastes!
We gather strength for the final push—
Over big, bruising, charcoal-colored granite boulders we get to the
      TOP!

It's a stellar achievement for Han Soo and me!
      We three stand all together on Three Spirit Peak,
      Four thousand two hundred foot Samshin-bong San.

We breathe the brisk air and survey the calm scene:
      Mountain peaks all around fade to mist at the edges.
      Autumn-colorful trees climb the steep mountainsides;
      And our sunshine-kissed shoulders enhance happiness.

After stepping-stepping down-down-down for two hours,
We gratefully fall into our car for the quick trip home.

A Winter Wonderland

My mother, who almost never said anything negative about any person, place, or thing, said gently, "I understand that Wisconsin winters are really terribly cold." We didn't take my mother's hint. With Elisa, 3½, and Ellen, 2½, and no friends in place, we moved in October of 1976 about 45 miles southwest of Green Bay to Neenah, Wisconsin, so that my husband could take a good, though very demanding job as tax supervisor in the home headquarters of the Kimberly-Clark Tax Department.

And indeed the winters, the first of which started soon after we arrived, were "really terribly cold." A good day was ten degrees above zero to ten below, although we sometimes had 25 degrees below zero with wind chills of 75 below. When snow started, usually in November, it just kept falling—and we kept shoveling—until maybe March, the "Month of the Black Snow" when our snow banks were not so constantly refreshed. Our 36-mile by 12-mile Lake Winnebago froze from Appleton at the top through Neenah and Oshkosh in the middle to Fond du Lac at the bottom. Sometimes we could hear booming as the ice shifted. Sometimes big cracks opened under the snow, and deer or dogs or even people fell in. Sometimes an ice boat, zipping along under sail, ran out of ice and plunged into open water. Sometimes a car or truck drove on the lake ice too close to the thinly iced Fox River entrance and sank into the lake. Most people survived, though many suffered hypothermia. Sometimes the ice broke up as late as mid-April.

Wow! Wisconsin sounds pretty brutal, right? Then why do I consider my 23 Wisconsin winters (along with 23 Wisconsin summers) to be the best time in my life? For one thing, we bundled up and toughened up: At three and four, Elisa and Ellen skated with us on park and schoolyard ice skating rinks made by firemen spraying water on rinks with packed snow edges; at grade school lunchtimes they continued this exercise. At five and six they cross-country skied with us on groomed trails through woodlands; at seven and eight they downhill skied with us on lovely swooping hills up north. In high school when it was zero degrees, they ran with no coats on between buildings carrying books and instruments. K-12 they almost never had school snow days.

We loved to ice skate on the pre-snow silken-smooth lake ice and sometimes see a live fish swimming under 18" of ice and to sled or tube down hills when the snow did come. Elisa brought her friend home from their college in Massachusetts to skate on the lake, and Ellen brought her East Coast friends home from their university in Chicago to experience the February Sturgeon Festival: a hundred cars driven onto Lake Winnebago, a hundred small houses erected over fishing holes drilled into the 18-24 inch-thick ice, a hundred people hunched over those holes waiting to harpoon—yes, *harpoon*—ugly, ancient sturgeons with the top prize usually going to a fish over five feet long weighing over 100 pounds. Meanwhile, the rest of us kept warm and amused in the big tent on the ice with hot brats, cold beer, and a lively polka band.

At Thanksgiving for many years our daughters and their neighborhood friends went from house to house, sang Christmas carols, and had each family draw the name of another family. For the weeks before Christmas, the children as Secret Santas—or *Krist Kindl*, the Christ Child—would leave gifts at the doors of their chosen families, not really so secretly because their tracks in the snow usually gave them away. All was revealed at a pre-Christmas party. And we winterized the Southwest custom of *lumenaria:* Instead of sand, we filled dozens of small paper bags with snow, stuck a candle in each one, lined the bags along the street and up our driveway and walk, and lit them at dark on Christmas Eve. They burned for hours, sometimes all night. Our kids called them "Santa's landing lights," and we loved walking the many beautifully lit neighborhood streets, breathing in the clear, frosty air, and meeting friends along the way.

I could go on and on, but you undoubtedly know my conclusion already. Despite the brutally cold Wisconsin environment, my family and I usually felt warm—warm from exhilarating exercise, stimulating activities, and heart-filling friendships.

I can shake off everything as I write;
my sorrows disappear, my courage is reborn.

Anne Frank

Joan (Corkie) Kirkham

Born in southern Indiana, Corkie grew up in Louisville, Kentucky, and acquired her nickname from a third grade friend who said her hair was the same color as her cocker spaniel, Corky. Joan's mother was not pleased.

Educated in Louisville, Boston and Kansas City, Corkie started work life as the chief bacteriologist at Lahey Clinic in Boston where she married an army officer and toured the earth as an army wife and mother. Upon settling in the Washington, D.C. area, Corkie started what would have become Angie's list had there been internet at that time. Out of that company, LEMMEDOIT, INC., came six restaurants and a bakery before she retired.

She now splits her time between Colorado Springs, where her daughter and family reside and a Romney, West Virginia, country place where she lives in a barn.

Only violent sea-sickness prevents her from her dream trip of sailing around the globe.

Dear Diary

1957. Met some new people today. She's a Brit. Very Brit. Pamela. He's a West Point Rhodes Scholar and six month old round faced baby girl. Pamela is having difficulty understanding American ways. Was astonished that nuts came in packages without their shells. This is going to be interesting.

Took walk with Pamela and baby today. Overcast and cold. Baby bouncing all over in stroller and hanging on for dear life. Was vigorous hike. Red cheeks all around.

Taking turns making Sunday breakfast. Pamela a whiz at waffles.

Went on another trek with Pamela and baby in stroller. Baby bouncing all over the place again but doesn't seem to mind. This is like going on a hunt without a horse.

Found out today that Pamela is Scottish! Yea! So happy she's not Irish. Granny always talks as if the Irish are subhuman.

Pat and I babysat baby today and dyed her hair red. Daddy was mad as a hornet but Pamela not so much. Guess that ends our babysitting.

Well guess what. Pamela went to Oxford and read law. Have a feeling that she would be defending circus people rather than corporate stuff had she finished.

1967. Pamela has taken up cigar smoking! I don't mind it because it reminds me of Grandfather. Oh well. Cigarette smoking is so common and pipes make such a mess.

1977. Dinner at Pamela's. Salad was a disaster. To dry the greens either she or son put them in a pillow case and into the dryer. Ruined the pillowcase and pureed the salad greens. Probably should have tried the delicate cycle.

1988. Dinner at Pat and Herb's. Pat saw a picture of a lobster platter that was a work of art and set out to replicate it. Think it took her about 4 days of gathering and cooking. When Pat presented it to the table tonight, Pamela exclaimed, "Oh Pat! It's beautiful! It must have taken you all of 2 hours!" The look on Pat's face was priceless and this will keep us amused for years to come, I'll bet.

1995. Pamela is getting a new hip. About time. You can see the pain in her face.

2004. Pamela called asking for my shrimp fettuccine recipe. Firstly, she said she didn't have any shrimp but she did have scallops and would they do. I said while they were both sea creatures, I wasn't even sure they were cousins. Then she said she didn't have the spice but she did have whatever. And—get this—she really didn't care for noodles and that I did know how she loved potatoes so she was going to serve it on mashed potatoes! I have told her time and time again not to voice her love of potatoes so loudly for fear people would think she was Irish! *Then* she said she would be sure to give me credit for the recipe at her dinner party! Lord, just take me now.

2014. Every year lately Pamela and I have been having the same conversation enumerating our physical losses. Geez.

2015. Pamela has developed a love of rhubarb pie and attempted to make one. Diary, I should post a picture but taking a photo of whatever that was on my plate would have been so.....well, Irish.

Gina Montepulciano

Secretly—OK. It was only a secret because it had been lingering and unspoken that she wanted to be Italian. To belong to a big happy loving fighting noisy family, that passion about everything, the music, the dancing, the festivals, the food, the piles and steaming heaps of food...she didn't know exactly the moment she felt this way. Who doesn't love spaghetti after all? She didn't look Italian, being blonde, blue-eyed WASP of a lass. Very Northern Italian perhaps. And very much not Catholic. No Catholics in her family. No Jews, No Arabs, no color other than white not that there was prejudice, that's just the way it was.

There was a time when she was maybe six that she had wanted to be a dandelion seed and float on the wind but that passed and she thought being a horse doctor might be nice but the sheer size of her patients was off-putting. Then an actor. She could be anyone or anything given the parts in elementary school where you were plants, trees and an occasional building or rock.

Sometimes when going to a party where she knew no one but the host or hostess, she would introduce herself as Gina Montepulciano partly because she liked to say, "Montepulciano." She stopped short of faking an accent but to be Italian for a couple of hours gave her great pleasure. She even concocted a family and family business. Nauga hides. Her family raised naugas but business had not been very good during the past years and the family was thinking about releasing the remaining naugas back into the wild and growing artichokes.

Her fake brother, Giovanni, was a violinist, her sister Donatella was a clothing designer, baby sister was a budding artist. What did Gina do? "I am a free-lance travel writer" she would answer. Not often but upon occasion someone would shout "Gina!" from across the street and it would take a second or two to respond. At least she knew where they'd met.

It's not that she didn't like her family but she was an only child of an only child of an only child and they could hold a reunion in the hall closet. Oh they would laugh and tease but it never would be anything that would cause the neighbors to call the police.

When she told a friend she thought she would learn to speak Italian, the friend asked why she would want to learn to speak a language only spoken in one country...try Spanish where, except for Brazil, a whole continent speaks it plus Spain and some islands someplace.

Gina replied that Italian was so expressive! You could convey such feeling! Italians have opera—olive oil—Gina had a friend (non-Italian) who met a Swiss man on an airplane. He owns an olive grove in Tuscany where they married and gave as a gift in the swag bag, bottles of their own olive oil. How cool was that?

Italians have their own salad dressing. Russians, French, Greek...what do we have—Ranch?

Italians have a boatload of history. Julius Caesar, Rome. Sicily Vesuvius, Michelangelo, Da Vinci, the Pope...who wouldn't want to be Italian?

The vineyards and the wine...she had read a book where the writer woman went to Tuscany, bought an old farm, renovated it, met a handsome Italian, married and presumably lives happily ever after. *It's possible*, she thought.

She had a pasta machine sitting on a shelf in the closet still in the box. One owner, mileage four (from Williams Sonoma to home). One step closer to being Italian.

On the internet, there were sites on how to become a Catholic in 34 weeks without going to church and then there were pasta making classes. And Match.com.

To Do List:

1. Learn to make pasta

2.

Eight Minutes

The nurse said that after she was unhooked from the respirator, the IVs and cleaned up, it would be eight minutes. Eight long, long minutes. Time to summon a minister, time for the granddaughter to sing a hymn, time for the brother, the sister, the grandchildren to say goodbye, say that they would be fine, that she could go, that they all loved her. Time for the minister to speak some comforting words to ease the patient into the next life.

The doctor had come to the family saying that it was time to let go. Her kidneys were failing, she was on a respirator, she was getting bed sores. Eight minutes.

The train from NY will arrive at Union Station in eight minutes. Watch the upcoming escalator for eight minutes. Joyous anticipation.

How long does it take to ski down this mountain? Blinding sun, bitter cold, stinging lungs—moguls—hard on the knees. Eight minutes to the bottom.

The baby's due. Water broke. Contractions contractions! In eight minutes? OMG OMG OMG OMG!

Sun, sand, ocean breeze, shade from the umbrella. "Eight minutes then time's up!"

"No, Mommy! Fifteen!"

Joan Kirkham

Home

Oh
how
happy
I
am
to
be
HOME!
That
place
was
AWFUL
Mommy
and
smelled
like
medicine
and
even
tho
they
said
it
was
a
condo
it
was
a
CAGE

And
It
was
so
noisy
I
Hardly
Slept
A
Wink
and
you
were
gone
FOREVER
and
I
thought
you
were
NEVER
coming
back
and
did
you
know
there
were
DOGS
there

Mommy
Dogs
have
no
manners
at
all
you
know
and
they
bark
bark
bark
all
the
time
and
Mommy
please
please
promise
me
that
we'll
never
ever
get
a
dog
because

Joan Kirkham

dogs
are
just
so
gross
and
they
said
you
had
left
my
favorite
food
but
even
the
water
didn't
taste
good
and
I
was
just
so
unhappy
Mommy
Mommy
Please
Stop

walking

around

unpacking

and

go

to

bed

so

I

can

curl

up

beside

you

and

put

my

head

on

your

shoulder

and

tell

you

how

happy

I

am

to

be

HOME!

Acknowledgements

The original landscape of the Peak was designed and painted specifically for this book by Rosemary Scheuering. Appreciation also goes to our supportive family and friends many of whom trudged through our early drafts. We owe thanks to one another for providing the encouragement to write. Creating this book has been an intense and gratifying joint effort which would have been daunting individually. We celebrate the present and anticipate the future as our voices continue to intersect beneath the Peak.